Wayne Frye spins a tale of adventure and romance that has long been forgotten by historians. Through meticulous research and the appropriation of previous yarns that map out details of a time in the life of Jim Bowie that solidified his legend, herein Frye puts pieces of a complicated puzzle together in order to bring history to life.

Like his works of fiction, Frye, in exploring the famous brawl on the sandbar in Vidalia, Louisiana enthrals the reader in what was one of the many incidents which would make Jim Bowie famous. Most people know of Bowie's death at the Alamo, but long before that he had made a name for himself as a gambler, a ladies man and a con-artist supreme who could rival Donald Trump.

Outwardly a gentleman, within he had a raging temper. In the incident at Vidalia, he would prove his mettle; prove that he was a man without fear, and above all, a man who could endure pain and near death to deliver a retributive blow against any individual who wronged him.

Add to the above his romance with Judalon de Bornay, and you have all the elements of another Frye thriller this time based on fact rather than fiction. Take a journey to New Orleans at a time when it was more French and Spanish, more Creole than American, and you have all the elements that make for a rousing adventure that truly makes the praise of one European critic who declared Frye the *Rembrandt of words* an accurate prediction for excitement.

Jim Bowie with his famous knife by his side.

Acadia Plantation in Thibodaux, Louisiana was Jim Bowie's home. It was demolished in 2010.

JIM BOWIE:
THE VIDALIA
SANDBAR BRAWL
AND
THE JUDALON
AFFAIR

By
J. Wayne Frye

A Historical Tale
Oft Forgotten in the Annals of Time.
Retold From Previous Accounts.

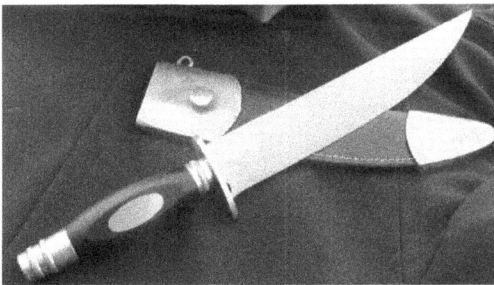

One of the Famous Bowie Knives

This book is written in Canadian English, so teachers should
alert students to the differences in spelling.

Jim Bowie: The Vidalia Sandbar Brawl
And the Judalon Affair

TO: Charles B. Atherley
"The Human Calculator"
(What grand times we once shared)

Also, as always to my muse:
Lynton Globa Viñas – the dynamic dynamo.

Catalogue Number: 971448-2021
ISBN: 978-1-928183-51-8

Fireside Books – Canadian Division
Part of the Peninsula Publishing Consortium

**Jim Bowie: The Vidalia Sandbar Brawl
And the Judalon Affair**

Table of Contents

Prologue……….7
Let's Begin Our Story
Chapter 1…….11
To Its Lasting Shame
Chapter 2…….33
Not Supposed to be Susceptible
Chapter 3…….49
Growing Legend
Chapter 4…….75
More Beautiful Than Ever
Chapter 5……101
Falling into Place
Chapter 6…...111
A Bit of Heaven or Hell
Chapter 7…..131
He Would be Wrong
Chapter 8…..155
A Mystery All These Years
Epilogue…..165
I Called It Being Smart
Sources……167

Jim Bowie: The Vidalia Sandbar Brawl And the Judalon Affair

ABOUT THE AUTHOR

Wayne Frye's *Aaron Adams* mysteries, *Chablis Louise Chavez* thrillers, *Girl* books and *Lynton* adventures titillate the brains of those who enjoy tantalizing tales. His life, like the heroes he writes about, has been filled with adventure and excitement.

He wrote his first book while an adolescent in Asheboro, North Carolina, but waited over 15 years before submitting it to a publisher. He has been a college hockey coach, professor and at one time the youngest university president in the USA. Called a marketing genius by the *Los Angeles Times*, he has been a promotional consultant to hockey teams and motion picture companies. He has been cited for his social work with gangs in Los Angeles and is active in the anti-globalization movement. A proud Canadian, he lives with his wife Lynton in Ladysmith on beautiful Vancouver Island.

Some of the 55 books by J. Wayne Frye

White Meteors and the Ghost of Sue Ann McGee
Hockey Mania and the Mystery of Nancy Running Elk
Something Evil in the Darkness at Hopkins House
How Hockey Saved a Jew From the Holocaust
The Girl Who Stirred up the Whirlwind
The Girl Who Motivated Murder Most Foul
The Girl Who Said Goodbye for the Last Time
Sammy Sasquatch and the Sts'ailes Star
Fall From Apocalypse
Armageddon Now
Worth Part 1: Roaring Through Life Like a Comet in the Midnight Sky
Worth Part 2: The Night of Thunder Road
Worth Part 3: Moonshine and Ghosts
When Jesus Came to Jersey as the Son of Thunder
When Jesus Came to Canada to Lead an Indigenous Rebellion
When Jesus Came to the Black Hills to do the Ghost Dance
When Jesus Came to Ladysmith to Battle the Angel of Death
Lynton Walks on Water
Lynton Curls Her Hair
Lynton and the Vampire at Tagaytay Manor
Lynton Buys a Cell-Phone and Hears the Voice of Doom
Lynton Viñas and Beowulf Perez in the Taal Inferno
Lynton and the Ghosts in the Mansion on Balete Drive
Lynton Viñas: Shadow in the Darkness
Lynton's South African Adventure
Lynton, the Karoo Vampire and the Jewels of Omar Bin Abi
Lynton and the Stellenbosch Terror
Chablis: Avenging Angel for the Forgotten
In the City of Lost Hope
Chablis and the Terrorist
Pursuit

J. Wayne Frye

Jim Bowie: The Vidalia Sandbar Brawl And the Judalon Affair

Prologue
Let's Begin Our Story

I am not herein going to make arbitrary excuses for Jim Bowie. He was, according to historians of considerable renown, a hard-drinking, gambling addicted, womanizing, hell-raising slave trader who, in my personal opinion, was an abhorrent individual. Yet, his name has been scribed into the pages of American history as a result of several highly publicized incidents, particularly for his death at the Alamo. However, there is one incident that receives little historical note that is actually probably his second greatest act of daring. That, my dear readers, is the purpose of this book; to lay out all the details related to what became known as the Vidalia Sandbar Brawl.

There is little doubt among the intelligentsia that Donald Trump will go down in history as America's worst President, but still around 33% of Americans bow before him as if he were a God. Add to that the fact that he won 46.8% of the popular vote in 2020 and you can make a reasonable assumption that racism is rampant among a large percentage of the U.S. population, as Trump made his racism blatantly clear; and thereby, more acceptable among his brethren. Jim Bowie also made no excuses for his oft practiced profession of slave-trader and his overt racism. However, Bowie never considered himself a racist, just a good businessman. He looked at black people as commodities to be bought and

Jim Bowie: The Vidalia Sandbar Brawl
And the Judalon Affair

sold for profit. Today, corporate CEO's enslave their employees in low wage jobs (another form of slavery) with few or no benefits to accrue riches for themselves and their stockholders. Of course, it is not just African Americans who are slaves in the great American bastion of capitalism today, but the poor working whites who are brainwashed into voting against their own interests through propaganda that convinces them immigrants and lazy minorities are destroying their economic well-being rather than their corporate masters. Jim Bowie was basically a CEO of his day, using his fame and financial position to his advantage just as today's American CEO's do.

Jim Bowie can actually not be separated from the time and place in which he lived. Born in 1796 in frontier Kentucky, he spent most of his life in Louisiana, where he was raised and where he later worked as a land speculator. His rise to fame began in 1827 on reports of the Sandbar Fight in Vidalia in Concordia Parish, Louisiana. What began as a duel between two other men deteriorated into a brawl in which Bowie, having been shot and stabbed, killed another combatant with his large knife. This, and other stories of Bowie's prowess with that weapon, led to the widespread popularity of what became known as the Bowie knife, which he did not actually make but did make famous. Even today the knife is prized like no other. In various forms it is produced by several companies with the best ones manufactured by the following:

J. Wayne Frye

Jim Bowie: The Vidalia Sandbar Brawl And the Judalon Affair

Ontario Knife Co.
Timber Rattler Western Outlaw Bowie Knife
Ka-Bar U.S. Marine Corps Bowie Knife
Buck Knives 119 Special Bowie Knife
Cold Steel Marauder Bowie Knife
Buck Knives 124 Frontiersman Fixed Blade
United Cutlery UC2863 Marine Force Recon

Although the Sandbar Brawl is the subject of this book, it is vital that there be some understanding of Jim Bowie to put what occurred that day in perspective. I have attempted to be as generally dispassionate and objective as humanly possible, but I must admit to some personal prejudices that, no doubt, will colour my interpretations of the man. With that caveat, let's begin our story.

Jim Bowie: The Vidalia Sandbar Brawl
And the Judalon Affair

Jim Bowie (Circa 1824)

J. Wayne Frye

Jim Bowie: The Vidalia Sandbar Brawl
And the Judalon Affair

Chapter 1
To Its Lasting Shame

New Orleans was not like any other city of the United States in the year 1817. Since Thomas Jefferson's great land purchase of 1803, it was recognized as a part of the young American nation by all the world powers, but Louisiana was not yet a state. New Orleans, however, had difficulty in so recognizing herself as a genuine part of the USA even after statehood, as it was seemingly a self-contained extension of Europe. Its languages were French and Spanish, while its manners, arts, cuisines and customs were Continental, not the more crude style of the American west.

Much like truly civilized societies today, the people of New Orleans, especially the women, regarded Americans as barbarians with a natural propensity toward violence and a generous helping of coarse manners. Yet, the greatest artery of commerce in the USA at the time was the Mississippi River which traversed through Louisiana right to New Orleans, heading to the Gulf of Mexico. Thus, despite is somewhat isolated nature; the city was exposed to the oft less polite elements of frontier America. Ships plied through the waters laden with wheat and corn, pigs and poultry, furs, lead, hemp, tobacco, anything to fill the great warehouses on the waterfront.

About this teeming metropolis of commerce strode James Bowie, a man who seemed to exude

Jim Bowie: The Vidalia Sandbar Brawl
And the Judalon Affair

supreme self-confidence with eyes that appeared to dance with delight that he was part of a city that then, and even today, seems more alive than many other American metropolises. Today, like in Jim Bowie's day, New Orleans may be a part of a conservative state, but it stands out as a hedonistic enclave where anything goes. There is a vibe to New Orleans that can be found nowhere else! Having lived there myself for a time, I can attest to the fact that there is a vibrancy to it that is, indeed, unique. I often strolled about the storied Vieux Carré and imagined myself back in the days when cotton was king on the waterfront and immaculately attired dandy characters strode up and down Bourbon Street about the balcony laden buildings with their wrought iron encasements where fine looking women smiled down at you.

I was young myself when living there, but I certainly did not have the swagger and bravado of the men of those times, particularly Jim Bowie. At 6:1 (186 metres) and 180 pounds (82 kilos), he was a truly imposing figure.

The young Jim Bowie stepped back to let the people hurry by, and could not help gazing at the marvels of this city with a back-countryman's unreserved delight. He was notably erect with precise posture, dark tanned skin, square chinned, fair haired, and with eyes that seemed to dance with hues of both blue and grey. Most put him down as of a sunny nature, but it was true that a man might get no more than a stare from him or a congenial nod. However, there was a countenance

J. Wayne Frye

to him that seemed to say, "Bear lightly upon my temperance." He exuded a blend of kindliness with a savagery near the surface that was not overtly evident, but each individual knew that it was best to tread lightly with him.

In the case of the Creole women scurrying about on this Sunday morning, Bowie conceded that their complexions were a plus not a negative: he had never seen anything prettier, in spite of the way they looked down their noses at an American like he was. Still, he admired the way they walked and held themselves in a manner proud and graceful and also subtly challenging, so that it was a pleasure to look upon them, as if somehow they made mankind more important and creditable merely because they happened to be a part of it.

He straightened and stood tall, close to a wall, as two beautiful girls went by. They were young, in their late teens, but women ripened early there and these were most beautifully self-possessed. About their feet their light dresses foamed, the tips of tiny slippers just peeping from beneath now and then, almost furtively, and precious to behold because so infrequently visible. On their heads were white shawls. Of the young man beside their path they seemed unaware, chatting lightly in French.

His eyes followed one woman. She was not even five feet tall, and entirely exquisite. A faint fragrance was left in the air by her passing, and he noticed that her waist was so slender his two big hands could have circled without squeezing.

Jim Bowie: The Vidalia Sandbar Brawl
And the Judalon Affair

A man came up to him and said in imperfect English, "Amercaine?"

In French, Jim replied, "Oui."

The man seized Bowie by the arm and said, "I need a man like you, a man who knows the wilds." Without asking, the stranger took his arm and pulled him along to a large home across the street and once inside urged him up the stairs where he walked to a room and almost pushed him inside, shutting the door behind them. The stench was such that Bowie was forced to hold his breath. Yet he glanced about him with a mighty curiosity as his remarkable host hurried to the window and threw it open to the fullest. Everywhere the walls were covered with paintings, finished and unfinished. Papers with sketches and daubs of paint were strewn on the floor and heaped in corners. To one side stood a rumpled bed and a littered washstand and by the window an easel. Now for the first time Bowie saw the cause of the dreadful odour. Near the easel, dead and putrefying, yet held upright on its long legs in some semblance of life's erectness by an ingenious system of wires, was a swamp heron.

"Alas," wailed the artist, "I kept et too long!" Almost tenderly he disengaged the disgusting carcass from its wire braces and threw it into the alley below. Then seizing a feathered hand fan, he vigorously fanned the air to clear the atmosphere.

"The paradox of existence," the man said. "My heron dies, and rots and the mongrel dogs of the street presently will devour her. Voilà!"

J. Wayne Frye

Jim Bowie: The Vidalia Sandbar Brawl
And the Judalon Affair

His hands dripped above the wash basin nearby, but with his chin he pointed to the easel, as the dumbfounded Bowie finally asked, "Why am I here, sir?"

The man replied, "You are an Amercaine, but you seem a rare breed for an Amercaine. You seem a bit refined, and as an artist I thought you might offer an opinion on my paintings of birds, as I am sure you have come from the backwoods and been around wild animals with regularity."

A bit perturbed that he could be taken for a backwoods person, despite the fact that he was, Bowie stepped to the window by the easel where the abominable smell had somewhat cleared. There was the heron, painted as in life, her feathers gleaming, her eyes bright, the mirrored waters of her native swamp at her feet, tall palmetto palms in the background.

"Do thee like it?" asked the artist anxiously.

"Beautiful," replied Bowie.

"Then behold," was the reply and the strange man with a flourish of excitement opened the black portfolio and began to spread painting after painting on the easel before the window. All were of birds, and Bowie almost forgot the lingering taint on the air in his interest.

"Yee name? asked the painter.

"Bowie, Jim Bowie."

Smiling as he extended his hand, the painter said, "And I am John."

As the two men left the room, gently was the door closed, as if the painter wanted no one to

Jim Bowie: The Vidalia Sandbar Brawl
And the Judalon Affair

know he was there. Then they were startled by a woman appearing at the head of the stairs. She was a broad, dark woman of middle age in a laced cap and black dress that looked up at them with a grimly hostile visage. She immediately seized the key John had left in the door. In her plump white fingers she held it as if it were gold. The artist gazed at her with a ludicrous combination of consternation, guilt and anxiety.

"Good day Madame," he faltered. "May I have my key?"

Her harsh lips opened. "It is no longer your key, monsieur, nor is it your room."

"My paintings?"

"Will remain where they are," the woman said. "I may find them of more substance than your promises, which mean nothing."

She turned her broad back and disappeared down the hall. Bowie glanced at John. The man seemed caved in, shrinking, as if humiliated almost beyond endurance. His face turned white and he sat suddenly down on the top stair step as he said, "I am ruined. The work of years, my whole career is gone in the blink of an eye."

John's eyes filled with tears, and Bowie, unaccustomed to the emotions of artistic men of this type was more impressed perhaps than need be by his new friend's despair.

"You're a little behind on your rent?" he said. "Would a loan help?"

He drew out his wallet, but the artist rose with frigid dignity. "Sir," he said, "I cannot recall asking thee or anyone for aid. I only brought you here because you seemed an outdoorsman, and I wanted your opinion on my wildlife paintings."

Actually, the man was affronted! Bowie found himself apologizing for his own kindly impulse. The despair returned to the man's face as Bowie said, "You've got something worth more than all those paintings."

"What could be worth more than them?"

"The artistic ability to make others, as good or even better," Bowie said as he placed a hand on the artist's shoulder. To his surprise, it trembled. Intuition told him that the fine-drawn look he had attributed to fatigue might be something else. This shabby man, who painted nature with such miraculous fidelity, was famished, actually faint from hunger. He started to say something, remembered the man's pride, and thought of a better approach. He grinned amiably and offered, "I mind a Cajun saying: *A taste of salt makes perfect a soup, a salad, or a new friendship.* If it suits your whim to go along with a little superstition of mine, John, come have dinner with me, so we can taste salt together and thus seal our friendship."

What had brought Jim Bowie to the city of New Orleans was not shared up to this point, but to understand what happened at the Sandbar it might be apropos to highlight the 21 years of his life up to 1817, so that there is proper background on just who he was. Bowie was the ninth of ten children born to Rezin and Elve Bowie. His father had been

Jim Bowie: The Vidalia Sandbar Brawl
And the Judalon Affair

wounded while fighting in the American Revolutionary War. In 1782 he married Elve, the young woman who had nursed him back to health. The Bowies first settled in Georgia and then moved to Kentucky. At the time of Jim Bowie's birth, his father owned eight slaves and had acquired 200 acres (80 hectares) along the Red River. They sold that property in 1800 and relocated to what is now Missouri. In 1802 they moved south to the Spanish part of Louisiana, where they settled in Bushley Bayou. The family eventually wound up in Opelousas, Louisiana in 1812.

Raised on the frontier, the Bowie children worked from a young age, helping clear the land and plant and cultivate crops. All the children learned to read and write in English, but James and his elder brother Rezin could also read, write and speak fluently in Spanish and French. The children learned to survive on the frontier, ranging from how to fish, butcher meat and run a farm and plantation. James Bowie became proficient with pistol, rifle and knife and had a reputation for fearlessness. When he was a boy, one of his Native American friends taught him to rope alligators. During the War of 1812, James and Rezin enlisted in the Louisiana militia. The Bowie brothers arrived in New Orleans too late to fight in the famous Battle of New Orleans, and after the war, James settled in Rapides Parish, supporting himself by sawing planks and lumber, and floating them down the bayou to sell at various places

J. Wayne Frye

where lumber was in demand. In June 1819, he joined a military expedition in an effort to liberate Texas from Spanish rule. The group encountered little resistance and, after capturing Nacogdoches, declared Texas an independent republic. The extent of Bowie's participation is unclear, but he returned to Louisiana before the invasion was repelled by Spanish troops. Shortly before the senior Bowie died in 1820, he gave ten slaves and horses and cattle to both James and Rezin. For the next seven years, the brothers worked together to develop several large estates in Louisiana, where the brothers hoped to take advantage of rising land prices through speculation. Without the capital required to buy large tracts of land, they entered into a partnership with pirate Jean Lafitte in 1818 to raise money. By then, the United States had outlawed the importation of slaves from Africa. Most southern states gave incentives for informing on the illegal slave trader, and informers could receive half of what the imported slaves would earn at auction as a reward. Bowie saw the banning of the slave trade as an opportunity to make money. He bought smuggled slaves and took them directly to a customhouse to inform on his own actions. When the customs officers offered the slaves for auction, Bowie purchased them and received back half the price he had paid, as allowed by the state laws. He could legally transport the slaves and resell them at a greater market value in New Orleans or areas farther up the Mississippi River.

Jim Bowie: The Vidalia Sandbar Brawl
And the Judalon Affair

Using this scheme, the brothers collected vast amounts of money to use for their land speculation ventures. In 1825, the two brothers joined with their younger brother Stephen to buy a plantation near Thibodaux, Louisiana. Within two years, they had established the first steam mill in Louisiana for grinding raw sugar cane. They used sixty-five slaves for labour in their mill. Two years later they sold the mill and the slaves for a huge profit and started speculating on land in Arkansas, where they were involved in a major Arkansas court case in the late 1820's over land speculation. When the United States purchased the Louisiana Territory in 1803, it had promised to honour all former land grant claims made to French and Spanish colonists. Efforts were made to establish who owned what land. In May 1824, Congress authorized the superior courts of each territory to hear suits from those who claimed they had been overlooked. Among the claimants were the Bowie brothers, who had actually never owned any land in the territory during the time covered. They had actually forged the documents attesting to land ownership. However, the documents mysteriously disappeared before the case could come to trial. Thus, the Bowies were never prosecuted for fraud and walked away with what would be millions in today's dollars.

So, this was the background of the man who was taking the painter named John out for dinner in 1817. When they neared the French Market, close by the levee, a small, lively, wizened little man hurried toward them. He wore a hunting coat and sash, and his cheerfulness was undimmed by the ugliness of a scar that disfigured one side of his face and his nose.

"Jim!" he cried. "I wait for you."

"Got delayed," said Bowie looking at John, "This is my friend, John."

"Rene Allard is the best hunter in the bayou" continued Jim.

Nodding, John said, "In reality my name is Jean-Jacques, but it is easier for my Amercaine friends if I just call myself John, even when they can speak French like you Jim."

Jim offered, "Ah, so now I learn your real name. I shall call you whatever you like, because French, English or Spanish makes no difference. I speak them all equally well."

"John is fine," the artist replied softly. "It is by that name I am known in artistic circles."

The three enjoyed dinner together. John began wolfing his food like one starved. Renee also plunged heartily into the fare.

In the alcove to the three's left were young Creoles conversing noisily, with frequent laughter. Bowie became interested in a pair of legs which stretched forth from the end of the table, differing from the other legs in that they did not sport the prevailing high-topped boots. Instead they were encased in long, fawn-coloured pantaloons, very tight at the calf and thigh, with straps under the insteps of the small and shapely varnished shoes. He could not see the owner of the legs because of

Jim Bowie: The Vidalia Sandbar Brawl
And the Judalon Affair

a column blocking the face view, but part of an arm and a hand were visible. The latter, slender-boned, held a glass of red wine, which slowly raised often to the hidden lips in a manner somewhat erratic, indicating a fairly advanced stage of tipsiness. Bowie decided that he did not care for the fawn-coloured legs, or their owner.

John, who had taken off the edge of his hunger, relaxed gratefully with his glass, and began to tell of himself, his childhood. He was born in Les Cayes in the French colony of what is now Haiti on his father's sugarcane plantation. His mother died when he was a few months old; after which, he moved to France. In France during the chaotic years of the French Revolution and its aftermath, the young man grew up refined since his family was affluent. He played the flute and violin, and learned to ride, fence and dance. He loved roaming in the woods, often returning with natural curiosities, including birds' eggs and nests, of which he made crude drawings. His father planned to make him a seaman, but to the disappointment of his father, he was susceptible to seasickness. His father was disappointed but supported his interest in nature. John focused on birds and had a wife, Lucy, who was sweet and loyal, and employed at the present as a governess in a household somewhere up the Mississippi River to support herself and her children, so her husband might find his destiny.

All at once he glanced down apologetically at his empty plate. "Forgive my garrulity. I was

J. Wayne Frye

much hungered, and drink at such times always makes my tongue overactive." He looked up. "It will do no harm to tell thee that this morning I returned from a field trip of a week's time and my provisions ran out and my wife has sent no money."

As he sat listening intently to John, Bowie kept glancing over at the fawn-coloured pantaloons in the alcove, now stretching forth crossing at the knees. Still, John continued, "I accepted a commission to paint some birds for a patron. On the prospect of making enough to pay my rent, I made promises to my landlady, promises I could not keep, since I have not finished the painting and been paid, and I shall never be paid it appears, as this patron has skipped out because of his own debts owed to a vast number of people."

The fawn legs in the alcove drew up rigidly as if their owner suddenly sat erect. It was then that Jim Bowie was about to get a surprise.

The owner of the fawn legs was a thorough surprise to Jim. Seeing those pantaloons had convinced Jim he was looking at the legs of an attractive young woman. The fawn legs stepped around the corner and their owner was revealed as a furiously angry young man in a long, swaggering scarlet-lined cape. He was slight in frame, with a smooth, handsome face, though there was a sense of recklessness that permeated from his glaring eyes.

"So I find you here!" he said as he moved toward John.

Jim Bowie: The Vidalia Sandbar Brawl
And the Judalon Affair

The artist bore a look of painful embarrassment, with an almost furtive side glance, as if he would have escaped if possible. "Narcisse," he almost whispered in response.

"You find time it appears to drink in taverns with scoundrels!"

"I beg of thee; I was drunk on cheap wine. I did not mean what was uttered in a stupor, and my friends here I can assure you are not scoundrels."

"Perhaps you consider that your patent to make scurrilous reference to my father, to ridicule my sister in a public place not reasons for me to find you despicable and to perhaps justifiably demand satisfaction?"

"In God's name, Narcisse, please! This should be no cause for a duel. I am a man of peace, if not always a man of discretion. My respect for Monsieur and my admiration for Mademoiselle your sister and, of course, your esteemed late father are beyond reproach. I sincerely apologize most abjectly for this misunderstanding. If thee wish, I will make my apologies to Mademoiselle also and to your mother, of course."

Narcisse de Bornays' lip curled slowly and deliberately as his eyes glistened with rage. "You imagine you will have opportunity for that? The de Bornays open not their doors for apologies or any other bootlicking to liars and dogs."

Narcisse raised a riding whip, which he had in his hand, as if to lash the shrinking artist, but Bowie came to his feet, knocking over the chair behind him.

J. Wayne Frye

Jim Bowie: The Vidalia Sandbar Brawl
And the Judalon Affair

Those sitting at the table in the alcove rose and turned toward Bowie, dark intentions and anger obvious, their visages hardening with dislike.

"Messieurs," Bowie said sternly, "I do not know the reason for this dispute, but I do know my friend John desires no trouble with you. Be so good as to return to your table and let this matter be settled in a more appropriate place."

Narcisse de Bornay looked Bowie up and down arrogantly. "Who may this be?" he inquired of John.

"My name is James Bowie."

"So his name is James Bowie," repeated de Bornay. "An Américain obviously, since it is abundantly clear he is no gentleman."

"As good a gentleman as you!"

"In that case you should know that a gentleman does not interfere in what is no affair of his!" De Bornay defiantly suggested.

"What affects my friend is my affair."

"And if not, you make it so? Is that it Monsieur Bowie? I suppose it would be impossible for any Américain to understand, to actually comprehend the difference between being a truly refined gentleman and being a clown, a boor, a barbarian."

"Believe me, sir; you do not want to mess with this clown! It seems I owe you some sort of an apology. I forgot that the conception of a gentleman in this place differs from that of the rest of the world. And that here such a creature should be treated for what he is, as obviously in your own case, a delicate and pap-nerved softling, as pale, as pretty and almost as feminine as a female!"

"Monsieur!" His hand reaching into an inner pocket of his coat, Narcisse de Bornay stood erect and determined. In that electric moment Bowie remembered he was unarmed and balanced on the balls of his feet, waiting for the others to draw.

Removing his hand from inside his coat pocket, Narcisse gave a chilling smile. "I said, and I still say the Américain is a boorish lout. And such as he is, perhaps he should be taught a lesson."

From the inner pocket de Bornay brought, not a pistol, but a card case. Deliberately he drew out a small card and flung it on the table. Bowie took it up, experiencing a pang of chagrin that he had no card of his own to exchange for it. He read the name – *Narcisse de Bornay*.

"I am lodging at the Noir Lodge," he said stiffly. "My name you have."

De Bornay bowed. He turned, exited and was followed by the others from the alcove.

Jim knew what the card on the table meant, as did his two companions.

John said, "This is my fault. Had I not befriended you this would not have happened? De Bornay is known here about as a man skilled in the art of duelling. Do not let false pride, my new friend; make you risk your life for no real reason. I implore you to make haste out of New Orleans."

"It is not your fault my friend. Do not blame yourself. This is a man who needs his comeuppance, and I am the man to deliver it."

Jim Bowie: The Vidalia Sandbar Brawl
And the Judalon Affair

"But Jim," pled John.

Sitting back down and waving his hand nonchalantly, Jim, smiling broadly, said with a resolute voice, "Let us not spoil the evening by discussing the matter further. Good food, good drink and good friends are more important than an arrogant dandy who prances about like a peacock in full-bloom. If it comes to it, I shall gladly pluck his feathers."

They parted company a bit later and Jim, unperturbed, got a good night's sleep. In fact, he was still snoozing the next morning when he heard a knock at his door. Opening the door, there before him stood two immaculately attired gentlemen. Blinking his eyes, Jim said, "May I assist you gentlemen?"

"We are here on behalf of Monsieur de Bornay," one of them said.

Bowie nodded, motioning for the gentlemen to enter his room but did not verbally reply. All he did was bow.

The taller of the two said, "Monsieur de Bornay has empowered us to arrange terms in the matter of which you are familiar according to your satisfaction, since you are the challenged party," offered the man stiffly.

Another nod came from Bowie but no words.

A moment's awkward pause, and then as if it were distasteful to utter the words, the taller man said, "Our principal, monsieur, desires us to inquire in what manner you wish his apology to be delivered."

Jim Bowie: The Vidalia Sandbar Brawl
And the Judalon Affair

It caught Bowie so by surprise that he wondered if he had heard rightly. "Apology?" he echoed.

"Yes, monsieur."

"I do not understand."

"Monsieur de Bornay is a gentleman whose courage has never been questioned. Let that be understood at once. He also has let us say an unusual sense of honour, which sometimes induces him to act in an extraordinary manner, or so some of us feel." He paused, as if to convey to Bowie that he, for one, did not approve of what was to follow. "In this instance, he requested us to inform you that realizing he was intoxicated last night, and considering his actions, he feels it your due and his own also as a gentleman that he offer his apologies."

Surprised, Jim replied, "We all do things we shouldn't when we imbibe too much. I willingly accept."

"You are willing to accept the apology, then?" asked the tall one.

"Why I suppose so. Very gentlemanly of him."

"In that case," the tall one said, "we are to ask if you require that it be put in writing, or made to you verbally, in person."

The chilled formality of the two before him caused Jim to pick his words carefully. "As to that," he said, "for myself I require no apology at all. If Monsieur de Bornay wishes to retract his words, let him do so to my friend John."

"So, you wish him to convey his apology to Monsieur Audubon then."

Jim Bowie: The Vidalia Sandbar Brawl
And the Judalon Affair

Realizing that he had not known his new friend's last name, Bowie suddenly connected the name John James Audubon to what he had heard from some ornithologists over the years. Yes, he was the famed man who painted birds. He had been in the company of the great bird man and not even known it.

Suddenly, the shorter man finally spoke. "Against my wishes, he will do so. Are we through here, then?"

Again, without words, Jim nodded courteously his acquiescence. The whole affair was laughable to him, but he hid his laughter.

The tall one said, "Permit us to say, monsieur, that we consider this magnanimous of you, especially since it was the purpose of Monsieur de Bornay, who esteems Monsieur Audubon, to make such retraction in his own instance." Then they threw in the kicker. "Now, since so much is agreed between us, shall we proceed to the next part of the business?"

Once more Bowie was baffled. "What other part is there?"

"But surely it is for you now to name to us your seconds my dear Mr. Bowie, so that the place of meeting and also the weapons can be determined?"

Bowie simply stared. Were these young fools insane?

"Let me understand," he said. "Did I not hear you say that Monsieur de Bornay offers his apologies?"

Jim Bowie: The Vidalia Sandbar Brawl
And the Judalon Affair

"You did," replied the tall one.

"Then would that not appear to be an end to the quarrel?"

"Monsieur does our principal less than justice with a mere apology," said the short one. "He would never dream of depriving you of the right of upholding your honour against him at the full risk of his own life."

Astonished, Bowie said, "Please inform your principal that my honour is not affronted, and for my part there need be no meeting at all."

Once more they bowed. "We trust this is not merely further magnanimity. He is very ready if you so desire."

Bowie could not contain a broad smile. "If he must fight, I'll name you the time and weapons! The time is when next it snows in New Orleans."

"But it never snows in New Orleans."

"I'm aware of that. The weapons will be snowballs when it does snow. Meantime, present my compliments to Monsieur de Bornay, and tell him that I would esteem it a privilege to shake his hand and so close the entire affair, which I'm very ready to say he has conducted in a manner that does him an infinite amount of credit."

In Bowie's manner was a suspicious levity. His message, moreover, seemed hardly couched in the proper terms. Yet, the two men felt duty bound to accept things as presented. They bowed stiffly and withdrew.

No sense of humour thought Jim as they left, closing the door behind them.

Jim Bowie: The Vidalia Sandbar Brawl
And the Judalon Affair

Bowie left the building and strolling down Bourbon Street he bumped into a very respectful and delighted old friend, Henri Rivera, who had a black man with him. Slapping Bowie on the back, he said as he pointed to the black man, "I got me a prized nigger here, Jim. You running a pack of slaves on your place and this here fella is prime, only 20 year old. Let me sell him to you for 1500 dollar cause I got me a gambling debt I need to pay.

Surveying the black man up and down, Bowie, realizing that prime black flesh was worth a good $2500, maybe more, said, "Sure, I'll take him off your hands. Walk with me over to the bank."

This was the real America, not the idealized one so often promoted by the flag-waving patriots who want to whitewash history past and present. Black people were commodities to be bought and sold. Pure and simple, Jim Bowie, like George Washington, Thomas Jefferson and a pack of other bigots hailed as great founders of the nation were nothing more than scoundrels who felt themselves exalted above other men, especially black men. Bowie, like Jefferson, who imprisoned his twelve year old slave, Sally Hemings and used her for his perverted sexual peccadilloes, ultimately had six children with her, saw female slaves as easy prey, but revered sturdy male slaves as priced commodities to be bought and sold like any other product. This was the real America, not the sanitized version taught in school and Bowie represented that America to its lasting shame.

Jim Bowie: The Vidalia Sandbar Brawl
And the Judalon Affair

The Eternal Shame of America:
A Louisiana Slave Auction
(Jim Bowie bought and sold over 500 slaves
during his lifetime.)

J. Wayne Frye

Jim Bowie: The Vidalia Sandbar Brawl
And the Judalon Affair

Chapter 2
Not Supposed to be Susceptible

Bowie shared his quarters now with James Audubon, who was waiting for him as he returned from the bank with a new prized possession in tow, his new slave, Aaron.

"What ails thee, James Bowie?" asked Audubon.

"It just come over me that I bought something I don't need and should get rid of it. I went into debt for fifteen hundred dollars to buy a nigger I've got no more use for than a second set of teeth," he said as he pointed at the poor black man standing stoically.

"Why did thee do it, James?"

Bowie thought back. He had not acted entirely without plan. A sudden secret scheme had suggested itself, but he was realizing how hare-brained that scheme was. It was too ridiculous even to mention.

"I couldn't stand to see this nigger being owned by a brute. I treat my slaves with kindness."

For a moment Bowie stared at Audubon. An odd harsh look came into his eyes. "You don't understand me, I reckon. I took one nigger away from a mean man. But I need to sell him to recoup my investment."

Bowie was right: Audubon did not understand him. In some ways he did not understand himself. He was moody the rest of that evening and next morning as they lounged in their room after breakfast with the slave on the floor.

Jim Bowie: The Vidalia Sandbar Brawl
And the Judalon Affair

Audubon rose and went to the door as a knock came. De Bornay waved him away and entered. For a moment he stood silent and then bowed to Bowie. "Monsieur, your message was conveyed to me."

"Yes?" replied Jim.

"Though its proposal was frivolous, I believe I recognized the good will behind it. I therefore have come to express my respects."

De Bornay had a smile of peculiar charm: he was very different from the arrogant, drunk and quarrelsome man of the day before.

Bowie returned the smile. "Thank you. And I'll say, Monsieur de Bornay, that I regret my own hasty words."

"We will not speak of that."

Bowie gathered that the hasty words still had power to rankle. They shook hands, and De Bornay turned winningly to Audubon.

"John, I was a scoundrel! Can you forgive?"

They embraced and laughed.

"Will you be seated?" Bowie said. "I regret you must share the quarters with my slave, but I just purchased him."

Looking over at the slave, sitting cross-legged on the floor, De Bornay said, "I have shared rooms with far worse, sir."

De Bornay was surprised, then concerned as to circumstances of Audubon's departure from his former lodgings came out. "This cannot be permitted!" he said.

"She is within her rights," replied Audubon.

Jim Bowie: The Vidalia Sandbar Brawl
And the Judalon Affair

"You are a great artist. I shall pay your back rent. You need access to your paintings and a well-lit studio where you can paint."

"No, I cannot accept. I shall take care of things myself."

"As you wish," replied De Bornay. He then turned to Jim and continued, "Are you to be long in the city?"

"Only a few days."

"In such time as you are here, if you care to see something of New Orleans will you accept me as your guide?"

"Yes.

"Then, as a beginning, since it is near noon, will the two of you be my guests at luncheon? You can chain the blackie up here."

Audubon said, "I have many things that need to be done."

Bowie alone accompanied Narcisse de Bornay to luncheon that day. They settled at their table and the two men who had acted as De Bornay's seconds walked in.

Bowie saw a short, broad-shouldered man, with a dark, heavy face, eyes cunningly intelligent, and an exceptional muscular structure settle into the nearby alcove. Noticing Jim's interest, De Bornay said, "That is Contrecourt, one of the best duellists in all of Louisiana. He recently killed Orsini, the Italian fencing master, in the cemetery.

"A duel in a cemetery?"

"One place of many. Usually it is St. Anthony's Square, directly behind the cathedral, which is screened from the street by shrubbery and convenient for impromptu swordplay. If pistols are used, it is customary to ride out to the Oaks of Allard, where a stray bullet is less likely to carry off a citizen wandering unsuspectingly by." Narcisse smiled. "Observe the gentleman to the left of Contrecourt?"

"Who is he?"

"He is the artist John Vanderlyn. He's very famous in New Orleans, because he understands what our friend Audubon does not. That to succeed the artist must flatter. Audubon is too abrupt with people. Anyway, who wants paintings of birds?"

Bowie nodded. Narcisse sipped, and said, "Perhaps it is the lot of geniuses to suffer. Originality is seldom welcome in the world. But why go out of the way to suffer?"

Bowie offered an astute analysis. "Those who do not conform are doomed to suffer in a world based on conformity. I, too, have great difficulty with conforming to what is expected by polite society. It is probably my downfall. I am afraid our friend Audubon may be even more non-conformist than I am. "

"John is too touchy to accept a loan, though it seems not to occur to him that living as your guest is hardly different from borrowing money from you. He only loves painting birds. Still he was invited to paint my sister. Ah, what a painting it would have been. He could be a great portrait painter if he'd get his mind off birds."

Jim Bowie: The Vidalia Sandbar Brawl
And the Judalon Affair

"So, he painted Mademoiselle de Bornay?"

Narcisse smiled a trifle wearily. "You don't know the whole story. It was through my efforts that my mother compacted with Audubon to paint my sister. My sweet sister Judalon thereupon invited some friends of her own age and sex to form an audience at the sitting. It's frequently done, giving the portrait thus added importance as a conversation piece."

"And Audubon failed to appear I bet?"

"And so," de Bornay said, "with the de Bornay interdict upon Audubon, no other New Orleans family will have anything to do with him?"

"And he's lost not only his livelihood, but his life's work?"

Narcisse nodded sadly. "I am attached to him. If there were only some way to help him get back in good graces with those who could put money in his pocket so he could devote more time eventually to his infernal birds."

Bowie took a deep breath and said, "If the de Bornays accepted him again, others would also."

Narcisse laughed. "You don't know my family, especially my sister who had all her friends there to watch the painting take place. She was humiliated by John not showing up." He then rubbed his chin and continued, "Jim," he said, "shall we conspire in behalf of Audubon?"

"In what manner?"

"First, I shall present you to my family."

"You have some sort of a plan then, I assume. Right?"

Jim Bowie: The Vidalia Sandbar Brawl
And the Judalon Affair

"You can control your temper?" de Bornay asked anxiously."

"Let's go now and I will impress you with my self-control," said Jim.

The family greeted Narcisse with warmth, tingeing off into coolness toward Bowie as introductions were made, including the painter Vanderlyn who also showed up.

"You've heard about the latest challenge?" asked Armand Lebain, a family friend, of Narcisse.

"Colonel Claridge and Belmonte with pistols," said Vanderlyn.

"The reason?"

Labain said. "Cards."

"Claridge will down him," said Narcisse.

Jim was aghast at how lightly people in New Orleans took death. He saw it as extraordinary vanity. The *code of the duellists* these gentleman moved in made them actually contemptuous of death, so long as it occurred in the classic manner on the duelling field. Any affront, however slight and sometimes even unmeant, might send these cretins out to shed one another's blood: somewhat theatrically, perhaps, but nevertheless with deadly willingness. Yet these men were perhaps no braver than any others when death confronted them in other form than the fashionable and highly stylized duel.

Since the duel hovered about so large, it followed that New Orleans was a gathering place for those who actually practiced this weird code.

Jim Bowie: The Vidalia Sandbar Brawl
And the Judalon Affair

Jim was not used to opulence, and in this situation he truly felt out of place, and also found himself wondering where Judalon was. The room in which they had taken seats made Jim reflect on the probable elegance of Judalon. It was richly furnished in the Bourbon fashion, with soft curtains of French lace, some paintings of merit on the walls, and beside the window a great carved rosewood piano. The instrument was magnificent and it was the first of its kind Bowie had ever seen, but that was not what really affected him. It was a girl who walked in and took a seat at the piano. He had seen her before. She was that girl he had seen walking by him on Sunday morning. She had given him one quick side glance, and he had not been able to forget it. Oh, and the scent she left in her wake? The girl had fixed upon herself his entire attention and interest. Was this the terrifying Mademoiselle de Bornay? She looked the reverse of frightening, sitting beside the great piano which served to emphasize her diminutive stature. He was captivated by eyes wide and lustrously dark with wonderful curved eyelashes and high-piled black curls on a small shapely head. The beauty of this perfect creature was spellbinding. So much so that her mere presence would have made a church bishop kick in a stained class window in homage to her grandeur. She was captivatingly beautiful and she knew it!

It required an effort of will to tear his gaze away, and receive his introduction to Mother de Bornay who was hardly taller than her daughter, though plump in figure. Her iron-grey hair was perfectly coiffed and her fine dark eyes contained a faint hint of surprise at Jim's obvious captivation with her daughter, as if she wondered why her son had brought to them this specimen of inferior gentleman with a frame so huge that it seemed to dwarf almost everything in the room.

Mademoiselle Judalon Daphne Seraphine de Bornay fought back laughter as Jim blundered out some sort of tongue-tied acknowledgment at their introduction. She managed a contrived smile that instantly disappeared and she gazed at him with that singular expressionless look that mirrors neither curiosity nor expectation, but a judgment secret and withheld. Her attitude was completely graceful, arms slim and bare, delicate white hands lying loosely together down at one side of her lap. Her gown, of some delicate white silken material, was low-cut displaying cleavage that was enticing but not vulgar, and the loveliness of all the world was in the cleft of that bosom, half concealed, half revealed. The pose was almost too elegant to be natural. A cynical man might have suspected that it was studied and refined through years of practice. She knew the power she had, and let it be on full display.

"Monsieur Bowie and I," said Narcisse, to break the silence, "exchanged challenges yesterday."

"Truly?" The girl's face showed a stirring of interest. "But you didn't meet? Why?"

"Happily we discovered that the reason for our quarrel had disappeared."

Jim Bowie: The Vidalia Sandbar Brawl
And the Judalon Affair

Smiling delicately, she said, "I thought gentlemen required only an opportunity to go bang-bang or cut-and-thrust with a sword to spill a little blood and be heroes. Have I been misinformed?"

Her question was addressed not to Narcisse, but directly to Bowie. In her eyes was an equivocal little light, a playful display of tease.

"To tell the truth, mademoiselle," he said, finding his tongue, "we avoided fighting solely because I was certain your brother would kill me."

"Don't let him deceive you," Narcisse said. "He was ready enough. It was I wriggled out of it."

"You know your brother sufficiently well to know how much of that to believe," said Bowie.

The equivocal gleam disappeared from the girl's eyes and she smiled: a smile singularly brilliant as she patted the piano bench and said, "Come and sit by me." Then she continued, "You are sitting in a most delicate chair. I am afraid this bench is the only chair suitable for a man of your size."

Hastily he accepted the sturdier bench, vexed with himself because he was sure the girl enjoyed toying with him after his obviously prurient interest in her. She had no shame with her wanton charms.

Thereafter he sipped coffee from a tiny porcelain cup far too small for his big hands to properly hold, and listened helplessly to conversation in which he had no part: talk quite trivial, quite sophisticated, and quite witty, in so far as he could follow it.

Jim Bowie: The Vidalia Sandbar Brawl
And the Judalon Affair

A far more captious eye than his would have discovered little to criticize in her beauty. Her features were dainty perhaps, but her mouth was ripe with puckered lips that seemed to be craving a kiss. But most of all there were those eyes!

Judalon de Bornay was extremely conscience of the glances the visitor was stealing at her, and they did not entirely displease her. She was, in the wisdom of the affairs of women and men, a generation ahead of any of her contemporaries, with knowledge inborn and then sharpened by experience. She had matured early and been in society since her fifteenth year, accustomed to being courted, admired and attended by men, so that their intense interest had become to her a necessity of life. As for this young barbarian called Jim Bowie, by no means was she yet sure how she would treat him. But his eagerness to please was so evident that she was certain she need merely to bat her charming eyes to captivate him into slavery to her whims.

Madame de Bornay asked a polite question. "Do you care for music, Monsieur Bowie?"

"Yes, madam," he replied.

"You are familiar with the piano?"

"No, this is the first one I've ever seen."

"Judalon, play something for us, will you?"

"But of course, mother."

The girl turned to the instrument and played a short selection. Bowie found himself more entranced by the movements of her slender fingers than by the music she rendered.

Jim Bowie: The Vidalia Sandbar Brawl
And the Judalon Affair

"Do you like it, monsieur?" she asked, as she finished.

"It's grand," he said, then surprised himself by venturing a compliment. "I admire the graceful way of your hands on the keys, mademoiselle."

"What do you do for music in your own country, Monsieur Bowie?"

"Not much," he confessed. "Of course the Cajuns are great fiddlers, and some play the flute and banjo."

She studied the guest. She saw how he looked at her. Judalon knew that light in the eyes of men. Her confidence was enhanced. She contrasted her own small perfection with his greatness. Small women often find a peculiarly intriguing challenge in the stealthy game with big men.

Judalon said to Bowie, "Monsieur, we hold a ball at this house next Thursday night. Will you not come as our guest?" At his look of hesitation, she gave him her most dazzling smile and exclaimed, "But of course you will! The card will be at your inn in the morning."

Outside, Narcisse said, "My congratulations. You survived my mother's penchant for cutting down people she thinks are not in her league socially. Believe me, were my father still alive, he would have been even more brutal. Yes, indeed I congratulate you on your saviour faire. You had a positive effect on my sister.

"And she upon me."

They went back to de Bornay's Bourbon Street apartment, which was extremely lavish. Bowie's eyes darkened with interest when he saw a weapon with a jewelled handle.

Seeing his interest, de Bornay said, "An Italian poniard of the sixteenth century of the type used by the assassins of the Borgia's."

"And this?" said Jim as he observed a beautiful knife with a jewelled handle.

"A French dagger," De Bornay nodded with the satisfaction of the collector who sees his choicest prizes admired. "I thought you would find that of more than passing interest, as I have heard of the unusual knife you usually carry."

Jim instinctively pulled his long coat back and fondled his knife that was in a scabbard attached to his belt, as he said, "May I take it down?"

"Assuredly."

Bowie lifted the knife from the wall. It was single-edged, with a two-handed grip and a very wide steel guard. He slashed the weapon through the air.

"Ah, one can see you are a man with talent when it comes to wielding a knife."

Jim replaced the knife and went on down the line examining other weapons, stopping at one in particular to scrutinize it.

"This," he said, "is a Scottish dirk." My uncle had one." Bowie lifted it from the wall and weighed it in his hand. It was something between a short sword and a knife, its steel about two feet long. "The balance is bad," he said. "You couldn't throw it."

"You throw a knife, monsieur?"

Jim Bowie: The Vidalia Sandbar Brawl
And the Judalon Affair

"I have been known to do so."

De Bornay was watching him closely. "You appear to have an affinity for the knife. I have observed frequently such a thing. Some men take naturally to the sword, some to the pistol, as if they were born to it. Often they become great virtuosos with their chosen weapon. With you it may be the knife."

"Somehow it appeals to me," Bowie said.

De Bornay looked at the bulge to the side of Jim's coat and said, "Tell me about your knife."

"Ah, its reputation actually dwarfs mine I am afraid. My knife is not a single design but a series of knives improved several times. The earliest such knife was made at my brother Rezin's request, but I have refined it over the years. Yet, it is an ongoing project on my part. It is made from an old file, as sometimes told to those who write of it as if it were some type of super weapon. Despite all the lurid stories told about campfires, I have never killed a man with it, only animals on occasion."

"I have never seen men duel with knives," offered de Bornay. "Only with swords and pistols. However, I hear snowballs are also a grand weapon for a duel." They both laughed, and Jim bid him adieu.

One Thursday evening Bowie walked through the darkness to the Maison de Bornay with his engraved invitation in hand, half eager to arrive, and at the same time half a mind to turn around and flee back to his room where he had left his slave chained to the bedpost. He heard French greetings and some laughter. Then he was at the entrance.

A black house slave took his card of invitation. Another received his hat and cane. A third announced his name as Judalon and a companion came to him He bowed, receiving from her a formal smile .

"Armand," she said in French to the man beside her, "this is the gentleman who is the friend of Narcisse."

The man paid no attention to Bowie, brushing by him and heading to someone in the corner. Ignoring the rudeness, Jim smiled at Judalon, turned toward the ballroom and blinked. It was quite dazzling. He had never imagined anything like it. Under the blazing crystal chandeliers the guests laughed and conversed, awaiting the opening of the dance. The women filled the eye to the exclusion of the men. Bare arms, shoulders, and white bosoms gleamed. Eyes and lips were very bright. Light gowns of delicate shades made an ever-changing pattern. For these the soberer costumes of the men were only a background.

Narcisse came to him across the polished floor. "I'd almost given you up," he said as he looked Bowie up and down, surprised at how magnificent he looked all dressed up.

A man came up to Judalon and said as the music began to play, "Our dance I believe?"

She turned to Jim as she took the man's hand and said, "Excuse me please, Monsieur Bowie."

Jim Bowie: The Vidalia Sandbar Brawl
And the Judalon Affair

Narcisse said to Jim, "Do not worry my friend; I have reserved a dance for you with Judalon. I am sure you can do the Virginia reel."

"Are you serious?"

Narcisse smiled. "Judalon really loves novelty. Moreover, she adores drawing attention to herself. I've convinced her that with you she'll be the centre of every eye, the subject of every tongue. That is what she adores."

Bowie, who saw himself in the light of a sort of public exhibit to provide amusement, was tempted to leave at that very moment until Narcisse said, "If only out of perversity, my charming sister is going to be quite kind to you. When the opportunity arises, bring up the subject of Audubon, tactfully. I'm almost sure she will agree to forgive him if only as a gesture to you."

"Why should she make such a grand gesture to me?"

"My sister is unpredictable, but she loves to play games of manipulation. Perhaps I ought to warn you to be on your guard against her. She is a wily one, quite heartless, but that sometimes can make her a perilous creature for a susceptible man to be around. Are you especially susceptible to female charms, Jim?"

Shrugging his shoulders, Jim replied, "Not always, but your sister is indeed beguiling."

"Well, in this case, you're forewarned. Let her smile at you, and flirt with you, and be very charming to you. Your chance will come if you are patient. Remember patience is a virtue.

Jim Bowie: The Vidalia Sandbar Brawl
And the Judalon Affair

Remember the reel." Narcisse said as he departed, leaving Bowie by the wall, wondering over the cynicism of a brother concerning his own sister.

Bowie watched only Judalon de Bornay. To his mind nobody compared with her. Her grace and beauty enchanted him. The top of her head, even with its gleaming dark curls piled high, came hardly to the shoulder of her partner. Both round captivating shoulders were exposed, and her gown of sheer white crepe was cut audaciously low in front. Her full flounced skirt, fringed at the bottom with little artificial rosebuds, reached hardly lower than midway between her knee and ankle, revealing her childlike feet in high French heels, which made her appear on tiptoe, as if she might at any moment spread iridescent wings and fly away. She seemed at once innocent and daring, an intoxicating combination of opposites. Bowie remained rooted, missing not one movement of the girl, one single expression as she turned and curtsied and coquetted with her partners. Using every pretty trick of dashing, twinkling eyes and smiles she was a deadly little display to watch, even for a young man forewarned and not supposed to be susceptible.

J. Wayne Frye

Jim Bowie: The Vidalia Sandbar Brawl
And the Judalon Affair

Chapter 3
Growing Legend

Narcisse found Jim by the punch bowl. "The intermission is at ten. The next number's the reel. Come with me."

Bowie hung back bashfully, but he was excited about the opportunity to be in close proximity to Judalon. Judalon was surrounded by young men, and she moved among them, laughing with sophisticated exhilaration. Finally as they trailed her to Jim, she said to them, "What can a poor girl do? Seven of you and only one of me."

Smiling at Jim she said, "I believe the next dance is yours Monsieur Bowie."

Bowie bent over and took the small hand she extended. Then he was walking with her out to the floor. The Virginia reel was familiar, and for one of his stature Bowie was light and quick of foot. At first he danced by instinct, but within a few moments he was in the spirit of it and enjoying himself. Judalon held out her hands to him and he swung her. Long after he had released her, his fingers retained the memory of her pressure on him. He felt very proud to be dancing with the most beautiful woman in the room, and correspondingly grateful to her for extending him the pleasure when so many were vying for her attention.

The girl smiled up at him. His fine shoulders were set off well by his coat, revealing his bulging muscles. His curly hair was newly trimmed, and

Jim Bowie: The Vidalia Sandbar Brawl
And the Judalon Affair

his sideburns brought out the satisfyingly grim angle of his jaw. Furthermore, his six feet and nearly two inches of height made every other man in the room seem almost insignificant.

The intermission was the time for refreshment, conversation and flirtation. Ordinarily Judalon would have held court for a dozen men, but tonight she had a different fancy. She tucked her hand into the crook of Bowie's arm. Looking up at him, she said, "Let's go out to the patio."

Young men bowed as they passed. She nodded gaily, spoke a smiling word with one or two, but never halted her progress. Bowie saw disappointment, incredulity and jealousy on their faces.

"Here's a seat by the fountain," Judalon said.

Tongue-tied, Bowie took his place beside her on the stone garden bench. The moon cast their shadows before them.

To Judalon de Bornay every man was worthy of appraisal. She was very young, but already she had a well-formed and hard theory of life: a woman's happiness rested on her power over others, and that meant her power over men, since it was through men that women accomplished all things at this time. In fact, Louisiana law, until the 1970's, classified women in the same category as the insane and idiots. Thus she determined that her beauty was a ticket to respectability and a life of leisure through men. She was incredibly vain, and only male flattery was worth anything to her. Flirtatious behaviour was natural in her, and she

J. Wayne Frye

practiced continuously the art of making men do things, taking in it the same elemental joy that a bird might experience in brilliant evolutions of flight. Since first she put on long dresses, she had never been without suitors.

Judalon secretly believed she had been the cause of at least two duels. In playing rivals against each other, she had not really dreamed of such eventualities. However, when they occurred she actually got some perverse pleasure in knowing men were willing to die for her hand. This gave her a secret feeling of power. A girl must mean much to a man when he will face death because of her. And it followed that if men were willing to die because of her, they might be made to do other things also, things perhaps more important to her than merely dying.

So now she sat with Bowie and asked him playful little questions. It would have surprised him to know that the questions really were most shrewd and that she was studying him secretly and quite coolly.

He was, she decided, a savage undoubtedly. Very seldom had she encountered a man so unsophisticated. His simple wonder at her, homage not to be restrained, was too easy, almost laughable. Still, he was different. He would provide amusement, perhaps.

"I must not keep you," Jim humbly said, "Many men await the pleasure of your company.

"I care nothing for the dance," she said. "I'm tired of waiting for men to pounce on me."

Jim Bowie: The Vidalia Sandbar Brawl
And the Judalon Affair

"Mademoiselle" Jim stuttered.

"Judalon," she said. "You must call me Judalon. And I shall call you James, no, Jim, because you're Narcisse's friend and therefore mine!"

He was too overwhelmed to reply as the music came softly, magically and she clutched his arm, snuggling against him. His body quivered at the touch, and she smiled deep inside as she worked her magic to gain another conquest.

It was at that moment that Jim asked something of her but it had nothing to do with love. She was so kind and understanding he said, so wouldn't she forgive Audubon, the painter? Maybe even reconsider and permit the painting of her portrait by him?

She was furious and was about to cut him to pieces with mockery and contempt. But another thought came. He deserved revenge more pronounced than mere rebuke.

She said, "Of course, have Monsieur Audubon come tomorrow. I am sure it can be arranged."

Then she left him so quickly that he could not overtake her before she was indoors. He wondered if he had said something wrong, but in the ballroom she was all beautiful charm again, with a special smile for him, a special tone of voice. He was relieved and happy, and if young men scowled at him, he made nothing of it.

Behind him he heard in a whisper the cool, firm voice of Narcisse say, "You're doing well, my friend."

"Am I?"

Jim Bowie: The Vidalia Sandbar Brawl
And the Judalon Affair

"If I know my sister, she's delighted. This sort of thing enchants her. All her admirers are fuming with rage. She's using you to whip her hounds, and the hounds don't enjoy the lash. Well, you've made enemies, or perhaps my sweet sister has made them for you. But this is without question the time to press your advantage."

"I've done so."

Narcisse was amazed. "How did you succeed?"

"She agreed to have Audubon paint her without hesitation."

When Jim returned home, Audubon was awake and reading. "How was the ball?" he asked of Jim.

"Very fine."

"Monsieur de Bornay?"

"Kind."

"Madame?"

"Gracious."

"And Mademoiselle?"

"Wonderful! And I have good news for you. You're to paint her portrait after all."

"I am truly astonished!"

"She regrets the unpleasantness," said Bowie, "and asks that you come to her house in the afternoon." He paused. "That should tell you what she's like."

"She asked thee to convey this message?"

"Yes."

A long silence, and then Audubon said, "My poor James."

"What?" Bowie replied.

"I foresee great peril for thee."

Jim Bowie: The Vidalia Sandbar Brawl
And the Judalon Affair

"Explain yourself."

"I do believe thee be smitten with Mademoiselle de Bornay."

"You talk like an idiot!"

"Even an idiot could see these symptoms," Audubon said.

"Is there anything wrong with her?" he asked violently.

"Concerning Mademoiselle I have nothing to say. She is as God made her. But concerning thee I feel most gravely."

"I'm listening."

"This girl is trouble, James. However desirable a woman may appear, it can often be an illusion of desire."

Bowie gave a gruff reply. "Do you reckon she'd think a second time about a bayou man, with no real money, position or prospects, when she can choose from the wealth and family of all New Orleans?"

"May I speak with candour, James?"

"You seem to be doing it already. Keep right on."

"Women sometimes love to play with men. And this one is a great artist at the play. She is ruthless. Her effect is already obvious on thee. You were a hunter, strong, little caring for foppery or the other superficialities that pass for important in this hive of superficiality. Now I see thee affecting the airs and garments of a would-be dandy."

With the peculiar vanity of young men, Bowie found that the "would-be" rankled in his mind.

Jim Bowie: The Vidalia Sandbar Brawl
And the Judalon Affair

Audubon explained that his nature observations had made him cognizant of the fact that the nearer a man lives to nature, the nobler his spirit. He had observed the natives of the American wild. The closer the native approached the white man's civilization, the more debased he became. Dishonesty, gross appetites, immorality, disease, the whole gamut of degenerative influences worked out their will on him. But the native in his forest or far out on his plains was splendid, worthy of love and admiration, free of all the perverse elements of so-called civilization. The native was free. The white man only thought he was free.

Bowie privately considered that the few Native Americans he had encountered in Louisiana undoubtedly possessed all that Audubon named, with poverty added. On the other hand, his father used to tell of sufficiently wild natives against whom he had fought in Kentucky, and the old man had great respect for them.

"Return to thy forest, James!" Audubon said. "With rifle in hand and thy eye on the wilds, thee will be closer to perfection than ever in this city, turning out thy toes like a French dancing master and practicing the mincing fake gentleman ways."

"If I did as you say, what would happen to your commission for the portrait of Mademoiselle de Bornay?"

"I should lose it again."

"It means nothing to you."

"It means everything. Don't you see? That is the problem."

Jim Bowie: The Vidalia Sandbar Brawl
And the Judalon Affair

"Then rest happy. I'm not taking your advice." Bowie grinned.

Jim undressed, walked over and moved Aaron to a column near the entrance to the room where he wrapped the chain and placed a chamber pot by his side. He blew out the candle and rolled into bed.

Jim lay in bed thinking about Judalon de Bornay, going over every episode of the evening, and trying to interpret every action, word and look of hers in relation to himself. At times he tried to chill the hope in him by savagely confronting the facts. How could a young lady of her station and training think seriously even once of a man like himself? But then he remembered the dizzying evidences of friendliness she had given him, and how she had favoured him over all the others.

Narcisse walked with Jim about Bourbon Street the next day. He said reflectively, "You were a sensation last night, especially with the ladies." He smiled devilishly. "New Orleans doesn't often see a figure like yours. I believe that Judalon was a bit jealous over you, because so many other damsels were noticing you. Our little Judalon asked me to bring you to the house this afternoon when she begins her sittings for Audubon.

Bowie heard the buzz of talk before he entered the de Bornay drawing room. When he and Narcisse went in, they saw a half-dozen young women, all pretty, and an equal number of young men, chattering around Judalon, who sat beside a window while Audubon fussed at his easel.

J. Wayne Frye

Jim Bowie: The Vidalia Sandbar Brawl
And the Judalon Affair

Judalon saw them across the room and gave them a vivid smile. "Jim! Come stand by me. I need someone interesting to talk to while this tiresome business is going on."

He obeyed her, as all men did. Audubon approached his subject to put her in position, with an anxious eye to the lighting. It took him some moments, and conversation lapsed as they watched him coax Judalon to tilt her head, turn her body ever so little in his direction, compose her hands in a certain manner and arrange her dress just so.

Bowie forgot the rest of the room in the picture she made. Hers was a complexion that bore daylight even better than candlelight, seeming to welcome the sharper glare as a means of revealing its perfection.

Rapidly, Audubon began working, sketching the figure, then the face. Behind him there were comments as Judalon began to devote her entire attention to Bowie. She made him come around, so that she could look at him without turning her head from the way Audubon had tilted it and chatted gaily.

The light faded and Audubon suggested they conclude for the day. Juadalon walked with Bowie to the sunlit patio, laughingly complaining that her feet had almost gone to sleep from the long sitting.

He was silent.

"What are you thinking?" she asked in French.

"Just thinking."

"Thinking what, Jim?" she teased.

Jim Bowie: The Vidalia Sandbar Brawl
And the Judalon Affair

"That you're too beautiful."

"Such a nice compliment."

"You are the most beautiful girl I've ever known."

"That's nice of you dear Jim." Her voice was low and soft.

"Judalon, this may sound like foolishness to you, but I think about you all the time."

So it was out. She had him! He then placed his hand on her arm. She said, "Take your hands off me, sir!" She drew herself away and looked at him white-faced. "If you must hear, I never heard anything so preposterous. You believe you've come a long way in a short time, don't you? Well, let me tell you that Narcisse's peculiar fancy for you gives you no right to presume to talk this way to me. If it weren't so ridiculous, it would be insulting. Go back to the bayou you call home, to that pig sty where you probably live."

She gave a cruel little laugh and left him, pale with anger and humiliation, standing alone in the garden. Narcisse, alone of the young men, was awaiting their return. The others had pointedly excused themselves while Bowie was with Judalon in the garden. In one glance Narcisse saw from Jim's face what had occurred. At once he left the house with Bowie, tugging him along.

"I'm sorry," he said after they had walked a few moments in silence.

"Never mind," Bowie said. "I had it coming for thinking someone like Judalon would be interested in me. It was pretty presumptuous on my part."

Jim Bowie: The Vidalia Sandbar Brawl
And the Judalon Affair

"Not at all presumptuous, Jim. I think she genuinely likes you."

"She has a strange way of showing it if she is truly interested."

That evening Audubon accompanied Bowie and Narcisse to St. Sylvain's Gambling Hall. After entering the lobby where they were relieved of their hats and canes, they passed into the large dining hall, with wide portals opening to a lounge on either side and an entrance to the gambling casino in the rear. In spite of his unhappy mood, Bowie was impressed by the richness of the place. Paintings, chiefly nudes, decorated the walls, and the wood carver's art was everywhere exemplified in tables, chairs, and sideboards which served the various purposes of the place.

Several gentlemen made a point of bowing to Bowie. It was an acknowledgment of a certain standing he had achieved, rather than any indication of friendship. He had been a guest at the de Bornay ball. His friendship with Narcisse was respected. The qualities that induced one of the great families to accept this Américain were not perhaps readily discernible, but it was well to let matters unfold themselves. Meantime, since the de Bornays appeared to be sponsoring Monsieur Bowie, a formal bow was policy

Jim was greeted by two men named Cabanal and Lebain, and the duellist supreme Contrecourt. The manner in which these men had ignored them created a reckless feeling in Bowie. He began almost to hope that somebody, especially the ultra snobbish Cabanal would try to make trouble before the evening was over.

Audubon said, "There's your most esteemed tailor my dear Narcisse, Janos Parisot."

The merchant sat alone at a table, gnawing a turkey leg.

"He never gambles," Narcisse said. "Janos Parisot believes only in the sure thing."

"Why is he here, then?" asked Bowie.

"To be seen," Narcisse said.

A portly man made his way toward Audubon, Jim and Narcisse. He said, "Ah, Monsieur de Bornay I rejoice at seeing you."

Narcisse replied, "I present my friends, Monsieur James Bowie and Monsieur John Audubon. And this my friends is Mr. St. Sylvain, himself."

St. Sylvain gave the impression of icy greyness. Not only was his attire grey, but his hair and slight waxed moustache was also.

"Monsieur Audubon, your servant," he said. "Of Monsieur Bowie I have just been informed of his presence. Your reputation precedes you."

St. Sylvain bowed slightly. "I am about to open a table of baccarat. Will you gentlemen join the party?"

Audubon hung back. "I'm going, James."

"Good-bye then and please see Aaron gets something to eat if you will."

"I will."

Bowie followed St. Sylvain and took a seat at a table next to the casino owner, with Narcisse on the other side of him. Across the table was a small man with thin auburn hair turning white at the temples, who was introduced as Monsieur Jarvis. Opposite Narcisse sat a rubicund, portly gentleman named Lombardi. The other three players at the far end of the table Bowie knew: Cabanal, Lebain and Contrecourt, the renowned professional swordsman.

The rules were absurdly simple, somewhat resembling blackjack, which Bowie knew very well. Instead of twenty-one, the points were nine or eight, with nine taking precedence. Tens and face cards counted zero. If one had a count of five or less, it was well to ask for a card: if more, to refuse. Only three hands, in each deal, competed: that of the dealer and of a player on each side of him. After each hand the play moved up the table, so all had a chance to try their luck and pit their skill. But though only two played against the bank each time, all the others could bet, either on their own side to win, or on both sides to win against the dealer. The latter procedure, which required some daring, was called a cheval.

Experimentally, Bowie pushed forward ten red chips. Two cards slid toward him. He had a five and a three - eight. He turned up his cards. A slight buzz of pleasure rose from his side of the table.

"A card, Monsieur Jarvis?" asked St. Sylvain. The red-haired man opposite nodded. He took the card and studied his hand. "Six," he said, turning it up.

Jim Bowie: The Vidalia Sandbar Brawl
And the Judalon Affair

St. Sylvain glanced at Bowie's eight and turned up his own cards. "Seven," he said.

The gambler had swiftly computed the bets on each side, and since they were slightly heavier on the right than the left, took his loss on the latter to collect on the former.

"The bank is five thousand, two hundred," he said.

Bowie saw the idea of the game. He pushed out three hundred in chips. Narcisse was the player. His count of seven won. Opposite, Lombardi called for a card, got a count of thirteen, and lost.

"I'm betting five hundred," Bowie said, "a cheval."

"Right's not winning," whispered Narcisse.

"We'll see," Bowie said.

For the first time both sides did win. In three bets Bowie had taken thirty-four hundred.

"The bank," said St. Sylvain, "is two thousand, one hundred."

An impulse seized Bowie. "Banco. I take it all."

It was his privilege and took precedence of all other bets. Imperturbably St. Sylvain dealt to him only. A deuce and a three: a count of five.

"Another card, monsieur?"

"Please."

He looked at the third card and turned up his hand. Nine.

St. Sylvain pushed over all his chips. "The bank is exhausted. Your pardon a moment while it is replenished." To Bowie he gave a grudging smile. "Monsieur's good fortune is exemplary."

Jim Bowie: The Vidalia Sandbar Brawl
And the Judalon Affair

Narcisse was shocked into silence. Contrecourt and Cabanal frowned over at Bowie, talking together in a low voice. Before Jim was more than five thousand dollars in chips.

"The bank is five thousand again." began St. Sylvain.

"Banco!"

"It is you and I then, monsieur?" said St. Sylvain as he dealt. At once Bowie turned up his cards: a trey and a six.

St. Sylvain smiled broadly. "The bank is exhausted again, and for the second time by this gentleman."

There were scowls and mutterings about the table. Bowie said, so that all could hear, "I shall propose banco each time in the future, if I am able to do so."

Contrecourt rose with a curse. "This Américain is making a nuisance of himself," he said.

Bowie appeared not to notice. He said, "Would you consider an increase in the bets, Monsieur St. Sylvain?"

"What increase?"

"I have here ten thousand, six hundred. I suggest ten thousand, six hundred."

St. Sylvain glanced about. Eyes, scores of eyes, were fixed on him, waiting to see what he would do. Every table in the casino was deserted to watch what was going on.

"What you propose is contrary to the rules of this house, but for this occasion we shall suspend the rules."

Jim Bowie: The Vidalia Sandbar Brawl
And the Judalon Affair

Narcisse sat dumbfounded. The crowd jostled to see. About him Bowie saw faces, Creole faces, white faces, hostile faces, and in their midst the hard glare of Contrecourt. They all hated him, hoped for his defeat.

Two oblongs of cardboard slithered across the table. He picked up the cards and looked at them. Ace and five. Hard decision. If he drew he risked breaking his hand. If not, the margin for his opponent was wide.

"A card," he said.

It was a trey. St. Sylvain drew almost perfunctorily. Bowie had won again.

"Twenty thousand, I believe?" said the gambler.

Bowie hesitated, and his glance flicked to Narcisse. Perspiration stood on his friend's face. Narcisse was worried. Twenty thousand and some hundreds more if he stopped now. Twenty thousand was good.

He counted. "I have here," he said, "twenty-one thousand, two hundred to be exact. Will you raise the limit again, monsieur?"

St. Sylvain had a grievous problem. If he lost again to the American he would be more than forty-two thousand dollars down for the night. A very large sum, and if continued this might mean the breaking of his house. But he nodded in the affirmative.

Philippe Cabanal, unable to stand the suspense, stood up and leaned on the table with both hands, chewing nervously on the end of his moustache. Narcisse went white. Complete, tense silence fell.

Jim Bowie: The Vidalia Sandbar Brawl
And the Judalon Affair

St. Sylvain shuffled and dealt.

Bowie turned up his hand. Deuce and the five of hearts. Seven.

Now St. Sylvain put his two cards face up on the table. All saw that he had a four and a king. An ugly hand. The face card counted as a zero, and since he could draw only one card, it must be either a four or a five to beat Bowie. One five already in the American's hand, and one four in his. In his mind St. Sylvain computed the odds. Eight to one in his opponent's favour.

He must draw. More than forty thousand dollars on the turn of this card. In all the room Bowie and St. Sylvain alone seemed calm.

They all saw the card as St. Sylvain turned it. The five of spades.

"The house wins, monsieur," the gambler said.

A yell of pure relief from the onlookers.

Bowie rose, and the correctness of his attitude was remembered. Not even an eyelash quivered.

He said, "I am finished Monsieur St. Sylvain, and I thank you for your great courtesy."

Narcisse, pale with anger, had made an inquiry directed at Contrecourt. The swordsman faced him deliberately.

"I remarked that it is a man's privilege to pick his friends, but that all privileges are susceptible of abuse. This American is distasteful at best."

In that moment Bowie knew that Contrecourt was dangerously bent on picking a quarrel. Narcisse was aware of it too, but in spite of the duellist's deadly reputation, he remained calm.

Jim Bowie: The Vidalia Sandbar Brawl
And the Judalon Affair

"Monsieur chooses to speak with ambiguity," Narcisse said.

"I will be happy to clarify my meaning," replied Contrecourt.

"Messieurs let us have no unseemliness in this house," said St. Sylvain.

Narcisse said, "Monsieur St. Sylvain is right. You will step with me into the garden, Contrecourt?"

So simply was the challenge given and accepted before Bowie could not even speak, much less try to stop it. Narcisse had taken this uneven meeting on himself because of Bowie. He could not match Contrecourt with the sword.

Bowie sternly surveyed the duellist. "You must be drunk, Contrecourt. This does not become you. He is an amateur."

"I am ready at any time, to demonstrate to anyone what does and what does not become me," replied the deadly duellist coldly.

Before anyone else could speak, Bowie was confronting Contrecourt. "You sternly mentioned clarifying your remark to Monsieur de Bornay," he said. "Suppose you do so."

Contrecourt turned on him, his cunningly intelligent eyes lit with some triumph, as if he were about to achieve an end he had planned. "Gladly." Most offensively, the duellist addressed, not Bowie, but the others about him. "I say that they fight as they game, a large display of bravado either cannot back up with any courage whatsoever."

Jim Bowie: The Vidalia Sandbar Brawl
And the Judalon Affair

Bowie's glare bored into him. "Who fights so, monsieur?"

Contrecourt could smile his contempt now. "All Américains."

"Any particular Américain?"

"If the sleeves fit, suppose Monsieur draws them on!"

"I do so. And I say here, to all, that this Contrecourt is a hired bravado, selling his sword to the highest bidder, no better than any whore who sells her body!"

An insult monsieur. Yet Contrecourt was not angry, so much as pleased "For that," he said, "you shall answer."

"Now, sir!"

Narcisse stepped between them. "Not until this man answers first to me!

"No, Narcisse!" Bowie said in his ear. "Don't you see that he wants me. You happened to have come between us."

Narcisse shook Bowie's hand from his arm. "Do me the goodness to let me fight my own quarrels."

As quickly, Contrecourt chose his seconds and then Narcisse chose his, one of whom was Bowie.

The crowd opened. Their party of seven passed out. Courtesy kept the others from pushing after them, though many went to the windows. The code was respected by every man in St. Sylvain's.

That moon, the same moon which had beguiled another garden only the night before now seemed only to give an added ghastliness to the present scene.

Jim Bowie: The Vidalia Sandbar Brawl
And the Judalon Affair

In their white shirts the antagonists faced each other. Narcisse slender compared to the duellist's powerful breadth was composed and determined; Contrecourt superior and sure.

Swords were brought, because swords were always quickly available anywhere in New Orleans.

"En garde," shouted Narcisse.

The swords sang their calliope of death with all the fanfare of a Beethoven symphony. Each pang of the blades sent chills through Jim's body, for he felt responsible for his friend's predicament. He saw the whole affair as pure senseless tragedy.

Narcisse knew his only hope was in attack. For a few brief, flurrying minutes, he followed thrust with thrust and his confidence built. Meanwhile, Jim looked on with trepidation. The sword fight is supposed to bring a sense of chivalry and fair-play, yet that is the stuff of noble tales and legend. On that night in the garden under the full moon there were no gentlemen, only long knives beneath the heavens, clanging incessantly as each man looked for an opening to snuff out the life of the other. The duel with swords was not the glory of King Arthur, but it was the darkness of life's end, the final curtain that concludes the play with dark tragedy. These were not knights duelling in embroidered splendour upon war horses that flowed over hallowed castle grounds in a contest to settle scores of truth. These were fools settling scores through ego-driven mania that clung to a ridiculous code of gentlemanliness.

J. Wayne Frye

Jim Bowie: The Vidalia Sandbar Brawl
And the Judalon Affair

The code by which these fools lived when the rest couldn't find their way to nobility made them prisoners of a past when they assumed bravery was a whisper of respect that somehow made them grand. They had their shining armour and the most glorious stubbornness to stand up for what was right, so they thought. They never saw themselves as mortal men, but they saw themselves as gods of chivalry, the ones who took the tongues of tyranny and rammed them back down their protagonists' throats. Ah, what fools thought Jim.

Fearful for his new-found friend, Jim fought the urge to barge between them, to pull his knife and show Contrecourt what a real blade of steel felt like, a blade that could gut a man with one strong parry.

Then the inevitable occurred. The professional swordsman saw his opening and lunged. Back staggered Narcisse. Strange, how the mortal sickness he felt showed in every line of his back as his sword clattered on the gravel walk. Bowie ran quickly and caught him. Even before he eased his friend to the ground, he knew. A wide descending curtain of blood sheeted the white silk shirt. Narcisse looked up with a question in his eyes, a question veiling itself in death. He coughed up a mouthful of blood, his slim young legs twisted in one sudden contortion of pain. He was gone.

Bowie laid the lifeless head upon a coat and rose. The seconds crowded about the stricken man. Contrecourt had not left his place. He stood, the point of his naked sword on the ground, watching the kneeling, stooping group, his face set and still in the moonlight.

"You killed him!" cried someone.

"I am sorry. I would have preferred to wound him only. But these hot-headed fools must take their medicine."

"By heaven, you'll answer for this to me, Contrecourt," said one of Narcisse's friends.

Contrecourt smiled coldly and detached, replying with arrogance, "At your convenience, sir."

The man had courage thought Jim. He had to give him that. He believed in himself, absolutely.

"At once then" offered the challenger.

"Your pardon," Bowie said. "Contrecourt meets me first."

"But Monsieur Bowie."

Bowie cut in abruptly. "I believe the challenge given me takes precedence?"

"Oui, monsieur." The duellist was incredibly contemptuous.

Bowie's heart sank. Narcisse was gone and Judalon had disdained him. Every dream in which he had indulged was gone. A madness of despair descended upon him, cradled in the black depths of his depression, so that for the first time in his life he felt a desire for the end almost like a suicide as the final act. If he could kill that man, the finish seemed welcome no matter what it might be.

The duellist was waiting contemptuously with sword still in hand, ready to dispatch Jim. It was then that Jim said to him, "One of us is going to die tonight Contrecourt perhaps both."

"The weapons, monsieur!" said Jim impatiently.

Mockingly Contrecourt lifted his blade. "This seems to serve me well enough."

"I'll use a knife," said Jim as he pulled back his coat and removed his knife from the scabbard on his hip.

"A knife against a sword? You are a fool," Contrecourt shrugged. "It is Monsieur's privilege to choose his way of dying and, of course, the place where he shall die. Here, I assume?"

Bowie looked at one of Narcisse's' seconds and said. "Is there a room hereabouts, empty and bare? It must be completely dark."

"What are you suggesting?" said the duellist. For the first time his composure was penetrated.

"This: it is mine to lay down the terms. You and I will be locked in a dark room in stocking feet, to move without a sound. He who comes out, if either does, will be the victor."

Contrecourt's heavy face was suddenly filled with doubt. The suave swordsman, this killer, did not too greatly value his life. Yet, in the thought of groping through blackness for an antagonist he discovered something that failed to appeal to him.

He fell back on ridicule. "What outlandishly insane rules are these? A barbarous backwoods custom, perhaps? An illustration of this man's vulgarity? No gentleman would suggest it!"

All at once, a rich, roaring laugh came from Jim. "Afraid?"

Jim Bowie: The Vidalia Sandbar Brawl
And the Judalon Affair

"Steel in the dark! This I like!" shouted someone nearby. You must agree, monsieur, it is within the right of the man challenged to name the place."

"Then you Contrecourt will either apologize to me or abide by these conditions. My friend, do you wish to eat your words?"

Contrecourt angrily shook his head.

"In that case," Jim said, "we will proceed.

They carried the poor limp body of Narcisse inside, and Bowie's mood of doom grew cold, ultimate and conclusive.

One of the seconds for Contrecourt said, "At the rear of this establishment is a storeroom, which is empty and windowless. The very room it appears that we need. Messieurs, accompany me!"

In the blackness, Contrecourt crouched and felt behind him with his hand for the wall, something substantial and reassuring.

The door had been locked. Outside, somewhere they stood waiting, all those who had peered outside and seen Narcisse so brutally slain.

Contrecourt took a firmer grip on his sword hilt and wondered where the other was in that room. There was total darkness. All at once Contrecourt began to regret that he had elected to use the sword in this madman's combat. With the sword one could keep a knife wielder at a distance and kill, but only if one could see. How to use it when one was blind? In the blackness, all his trained lethal skill was for naught.

Contrecourt could face death with bravery. He had done so often. But this was outside of anything he had experienced. The skin prickled on his back. His shirt was wet with sweat: the sweat of nervousness and fear.

He held his breath, trying to hear the breathing or any soft movement of his enemy there in the darkness. But though he held it until his lungs seemed bursting, no faint whisper of sound came to his straining ears.

Where was that accursed Américain? From what direction would he come? Contrecourt suppressed an instinct to whip his sword wildly about him to keep off the creeping peril, but he realized the sound of the blade slashing the air would betray his position.

Minutes passed, trembling slowly by like hours. How long had they been there? Why, oh why did not that fiend move, or do something, anything?

It was not a sound, so much as the beginning of a mere guess of where a sound was. Frantically, he stabbed in that direction. Only emptiness.

At once he was fearful that the slight rustle of his movement might have told his position. He listened. Silence was absolute. Only the thumping of the pulse in his ears seemed unnaturally loud. He must find a corner he thought. If he could find a corner, with his back in it, the sword would have much greater chance to hold off that silent, inexorable enemy. Perhaps if he moved silently enough the other might grope toward the place he had just quit and thus reveal himself.

With infinite care, Contrecourt began the stealthy withdrawal. His body was bent, his sword half extended before him. In silk stockings his feet moved slowly and softly, not sliding but lifted and placed, touched barely on the floor at first and then gradually set down. It seemed the pounding of his heart must be heard more than any sound of movement he made.

To move three feet required an unconscionable time. Still no sound. Still the impenetrable blackness of the windowless room with its walls of thick stone. The corner, the corner. He reached out a careful, inquiring hand. This must be the corner.

Suddenly, with a scream he desperately whipped the blade of his sword around in the dark. Too late! There was a sudden dreadful pain in Contrecourt's heart side, and then the blackness of eternity, of death as he fell with the knife plunged deep into his heart. Jim bent over him, pulled out the knife and walked to the door. He knocked and to the surprise of all there stood the mighty Jim Bowie, victor over the man who had slain his friend. The story of that night in that room would spread all over America, as Jim Bowie added to his growing legend.

Jim Bowie: The Vidalia Sandbar Brawl
And the Judalon Affair

Chapter 4
More Beautiful Than Ever

Jim's last days in New Orleans had been filled with chilled bitterness. There was the death of Narcisse and his own fight with Contrecourt. He remembered the madness, the desire to die with which he had gone into that weird pitch-dark duel, and it was a matter for contemplation. He had never before known such a mood. There was a smell of sickness about it that he did not understand or like.

Then there was Narcisse's funeral. He sat far back in the cathedral, listened to the solemn chanting and watched the priest fling the holy water over the casket. He did not go to the cemetery. There was the moment when he stood before the door of the Maison de Bornay, hoping to express his sympathy concerning Narcisse, only to receive an icy message of refusal from Judalon delivered by the lips of the black butler.

With Narcisse gone, he felt empty inside. Never had someone's death so affected him, but his spirits were lifted when Audubon embraced him and watched Jim go sadly from the town, as if sure in his mind that his friend had embarked on a course predestined to unhappiness. So Bowie came home to the bayou, ashamed and bitter, to face a difficult explanation to his brothers.

His brothers came out on the porch and then down the path toward him, sleep still in their eyes. But the sleep fled quickly when they had a good look at his long tight pantaloons, his citified coat and his dandy of a hat.

John, the eldest of the three brothers, the man of finance in the family said, "Did you make our deal?"

Jim looked him in the eye. "No."

Then Rezin Bowie said, "What did you do?"

"I killed a man."

"Needed killing?" asked Rezin.

"Yep."

"I bought a nigger," Bowie said, pointing outside where Aaron was squatting on the porch "and signed a note for fifteen hundred dollars for him."

"You what? Fifteen hundred?" This transcended in importance the killing of any man as it was a steep price for a slave to be resold.

Aaron was called from the landing and examined from all sides. He was eager to please, his eyeballs showing white.

"You'd better be good," growled Rezin.

Aaron was dismissed and a silence fell upon the three as Jim felt guilty as he said, "I talked with the lumber man and his offer would break us. Can't sell lumber at the price he or anyone else was willing to pay. Lumber is in over supply."

"I argued," Bowie said. "No good. Finally he came up with an offer to buy us out."

"Buy us out?" They yelled angrily.

"Offered five thousand, lock, stock and barrel."

"What did you say?" John asked.

"I laughed at him."

Jim Bowie: The Vidalia Sandbar Brawl
And the Judalon Affair

"Good." John was relieved.

"I said we wouldn't take less than six thousand. What's more, I got it. I have the signed option right here in my pocket."

"Not much," said Rezin, "but we been going under for years. Best we take it and move on to something else. Thus, the boys sold out and readied themselves to become slave traders, where over the next few months they made $65,000 in the illegal slave trade.

The young American nation was gathering itself for its next great journey into the wilderness in the summer of 1827. It was a movement of population mostly spontaneous. Yet, even though unplanned, the inward urges are forever more irresistible than the schemes of statesmen, however far-sighted, ambitious or ruthless.

In that summer the frontier knew one of the great historical moments of opportunity. West of the Mississippi River lay uncounted millions of unoccupied acres, and a nation of farmers, thinking of wealth chiefly in terms of land, desired them. Men with courage and luck might get a quick start in life by plunging into the unknown. The families knew the dark loneliness, the privations and the dangers they must face. Yet they piled up along the great river all the way from its confluence with the Missouri to its Delta, and gazed across the muddy flood with hungering eyes.

At a place called Natchez, in July of 1827, the river front was covered with cargo boats, moored sometimes three and four deep, their crews fighting and cursing each other, a symptom of the complicated stirring of a people on the move. Night and day they had drifted, running the peril of raging rapids and of murderous river pirates. They slept and ate in sun or storm on the open deck, subsisting on coarse meat and bread devoured out of a common pan or kettle set down among them as if they were so many dogs.

What of Natchez? A city? No, two cities as separate and distinct as if they were a hundred leagues apart. Sweeping in a mighty curve, the Mississippi had carved out from its eastern bank a lofty cliff of white and gray rock, at the foot of which, on a narrow strip of mucky ground, stood a huddle of weathered shacks and crumbling brick buildings, stinking with evil. This was the only part of Natchez the boatmen ever saw. Here was the poisonous Mecca of sin and debauchery; here crime was habitual, cheating and violence normal, bestial drunkenness universal, death an incident, and harlotry the sole occupation of many women. Those women, hard and brazen, equal to any depravity, expecting no kindness from any man, but greedy for the gold of every man, were as good an index as any of the vicious population in that turbulent eddy on the river bottom. This was Natchez-under-the-Bluff, a city of sin.

Through the ruffian settlement, Silver Street raked its narrow course, crisscrossed by dark alleys, each a menacing cavalcade of evil. But Silver Street did not stop there. In a steep slant it climbed the face of the cliff, providing a link with the world above. And there, on top of the bluff, calm and secure, stood the pillared mansions of the rich cotton planters, with their velvet lawns and stately trees, the steeple-laden churches, the courthouse, the ordered shops and cafés. There gentlemen in rich garb, with stately manners and keen eyes, strolled or drank fancy drinks, or laid bets or dealt in slaves and cotton, or paid extravagant compliments to the ladies of their acquaintance whom they met. And here again the women struck the keynote: dainty women, dwelling in unmatched luxury and ease, waited upon by whole retinues of black servant slaves, attended and flattered and spoiled by courtly men, beautiful, idle, sparkling, wilful and very expectant of respect. This place was known as Natchez-on-the-Hill.

Of the villainous establishments below the Natchez bluffs, none was more villainous than Thomas Grady's tavern. It was particularly so at night, when darkness added to its filthy disreputability, and a few wretched human beings built their own winding shrouds of drippings as they threw fantastic shadows. All freshness was excluded from the place, so that its atmosphere was sodden and shamed by smells of stale liquor and bad food, and by the breaths and body odours of the rogues and vagabonds who haunted the place.

Tom Grady himself, a man of limited intelligence, still more limited scruples, and a paunch that could stomach anything, sat in his rawhide chair, caring nothing for fresh air, and listening complacently to the clink of glasses, shrill female laughter, and the overhanging cloud of obscene male discourse which assured him of his inn's popularity.

In the saloon and house of ill repute were five women and four men, excluding himself. Of the women, four were moderately youthful and immoderately hard and brazen. Mother Slappert's girls who made the inn a soliciting place sat waiting for paying customers. The fifth was the venerable abbess of vice herself, Mother Slappert, fat, cunning, and grey, with enormous breasts sagging under her loose dress. She had been beautiful at one time, but as she aged the outer beauty faded and the inner beauty rotted.

Four men played idly at cards, and the girls looked about disinterestingly, sitting on chair arms, leaning against shoulders, accepting coarse liberties with giggling complaisance. Grady knew the men: each was a thief and very likely a murderer. There was Joe Burke, rotund and bald with an evil visage that belied his figure's jovial promise; Buck Sorrels, a great harmless-looking oaf with a foolish grin, who was far from foolish and anything but harmless; and Steve Heacock, gaunt and voluminous, of the three appearing most truly the scoundrel he was.

All of these wore rough river costumes, part leather and part homespun. But the fourth, a burly, swaggering fellow, perhaps forty, was attired in a

Jim Bowie: The Vidalia Sandbar Brawl
And the Judalon Affair

Bolivar coat and a tall hat, which he wore tilted far over on the side of his head. He had a persuasive, jocular manner, in spite of a trifling oddity of appearance: one tooth in his mouth projected so that it required a constant little effort to cover it with his lip and somewhat marred his smile. This fourth man was John Sturdevant, better known as Bloody Jack Sturdevant. Grady knew him to be a murderous fighter with any weapon. Some said he was the strongest man on the river, a squat Hercules, who had killed six men in single combats. How many other deaths he was responsible for nobody cared to discuss. Ostensibly a professional gambler, an occupation almost respectable in Natchez-under-the Bluff, he was given to long absences, and Grady, who heard everything, remembered a whisper concerning a man "with a wolf tooth" who bossed the upriver pirates who lay in wait for unwary flatboats. The saloon keeper, however, asked no questions. Bloody Jack Sturdevant was a good customer, spending half his time under the bluff, and at least nine tenths of that in Grady's tavern.

The door opened, admitting for a moment a breath of cool night air, and with it a tall, straight-backed man, who, unlike many tall men, held his head high and proud.

"Howdy, Grady," he said.

The innkeeper hoisted himself to his feet. "Tolerable, Mr. Bowie."

Mr. Bowie looked to be in reasonable good health. The years had put no soft flesh on his hard bone and muscle, but his eyes, however, told the most about him: they were grey and watchful, and sometimes cold and intimidating. The incident in New Orleans ten long years ago had hardened him somewhat.

Bowie was alone there, which argued for a certain self-confidence. It was not considered healthy for gentlemen from the breeze-swept heights above to venture solitary down in this hellhole, but Jim did it regularly.

The tavern's patrons regarded him with a variety of speculations. And if the furtive men mentally assessed his possible worth to filching fingers or perhaps a stab in the back, the bold-eyed women gazed at his resolute face and his shoulders with a different interest. But the men, after another scrutiny, decided to let alone such obviously dangerous competence: and the women perceived that as far as this gentleman was concerned, they existed not at all. He pursued more stately women.

Grady set a bottle on the bar, but Bowie shook his head. The gents rose, shook off the arms of their girls, and tramped over. With a kind of robust polish that became his style and appearance, Sturdevant bowed, and said, "Honoured to meet you, sir." The others only nodded sourly and stood back.

" Buy you a drink, gentlemen?" Bowie said.

They drank his good health.

"Mr. Sturdevant owns a fine animal you might be interested in," said the innkeeper.

"Could be. Let's take a look."

Jim Bowie: The Vidalia Sandbar Brawl
And the Judalon Affair

"Name's Steel Duke, sir. Know of the horse?"

"No." Bowie replied.

"Sired by General Jackson's famous stallion. I presume you're familiar with the line. The Duke's a mighty well-known stake horse around Nashville. Beat some mighty fine horses."

"I'll look at him."

Grady took a lantern and led out into the night. From a hitch rack Bowie un-tethered the horse, noticing that it had been ridden recently as dark sweat stains showed about the edges of his saddle blanket. "He looks choicely good. But I want to see him by daylight. Bring him up to Henderson's stable at nine tomorrow morning. If he's what you say and the papers are regular, the money will be ready for you."

As big as a bass drum, the full moon heaved itself over the black forest to the east and drenched the landscape with foggy silver, so swift and blinding that a man had to blink twice to believe it. It made the shadow of the bluff twice as black, so that except for the sound of his horse's hoofs, Bowie's progress up the long incline could hardly be traced.

As he emerged in the moonlight above, he saw two men conversing on the street. By an odd quirk of fate, one of those men was very closely connected with an errand from which he was just returning.

The taller of the pair was Andrew Marschalk, the veteran editor of the *Natchez Herald.* He was a thin, spare man, with silver hair and a cast of

J. Wayne Frye   83

Jim Bowie: The Vidalia Sandbar Brawl
And the Judalon Affair

countenance almost sorrowful, save when he chose to be winning at cards. The other was younger, nervous with a narrow dark face, very black hair and moustache and teeth gleaming white. He was Major Norris Wright, owner of the Irish thoroughbred Kerry Isle, and he was handsome, almost foppish in white leather riding tights and immaculate boots which he tapped continuously with his riding whip.

Bowie would have stopped to speak to Marschalk, whom he respected, but at the sight of the other, he merely nodded and rode on.

"James Bowie," said the major, looking after him. "He rides like an emperor, and he gives the imperial nod these days. I knew him long ago, Andrew, when a paper dollar was a fortune to him, and he didn't know good wine from rot-gut whiskey."

Marschalk smiled slightly. "Change is life, Major. Some men grow, and the spectacle of their growth is often a little disconcerting. Especially when it's a toadstool growth pushing up overnight, with no substance or value and with a bad smell to boot."

The editor did not reply directly. "Mr. Bowie appears to have been on some errand of pressing nature," he said.

"A game of chance on the landing, probably, if not a rendezvous at some sporting house with a female of dubious reputation! He is a man of pedestrian tastes whose reputation for good or bad, maybe both, grows and grows."

Jim Bowie: The Vidalia Sandbar Brawl
And the Judalon Affair

Marschalk shook his head. "I think you do him injustice. Did you see the sweat marks on that horse? He's come from farther than the landing."

Norris Wright laughed. "Even injustice is more than that man deserves, sir! A bog trotter, a slave-runner, a gambler and a ruffian, crooked as a coiled rattle snake, sir!"

The white-haired editor was silent. No man expressed himself, not even to an intimate friend, as Major Wright had done, unless he had notions of backing up the words with some kind of violent action if opportunity arose. And while Marschalk was an acquaintance of considerable time, he was hardly one of the major's intimates. As a matter of fact he was no intimate of anyone's as the austerity of his manner forbade intimacy. What Wright spoke so freely and venomously to him he would not hesitate to speak elsewhere. This sort of thing led to the shedding of blood.

Wright lifted his hat and bade all there adieu. For a moment Marschalk remained standing where he was. From below the bluff came the brawling noise of the ruffian settlement. The great moon seemed to hang in arm's reach, touching the wide river with a thousand highlights. Far across, the steam ferryboat cast a long path of reflections toward a low dark island near the distant shore.

The editor knew that island. It resembled twenty thousand others in Mississippi and Louisiana, but it had a significance apart. On the river maps it was called the Vidalia Sand Bar. But from the Ohio, clear down to New Orleans, every

J. Wayne Frye 85

Jim Bowie: The Vidalia Sandbar Brawl
And the Judalon Affair

steamboat pilot, raftsman, gambler, cotton merchant, flatboater and catfisher knew it as the Natchez butchering ground. It was the place of duels, where fiery gentlemen snuffed out each other's lives, paradoxically whitening honour in the scarlet gush of blood. Marschalk disliked the island and its character. A man gains perspective with age, and more and more each year he deplored every aspect of the so-called "code of honour" with its obligations and excesses. Yet when men set their heads to kill or be killed, there was not much one could do about it.

Major Wright seemed to like the word slave-runner used to describe Bowie. Not a pleasant word. Rather, a fighting word. Remarkable, he thought, that a man like Bowie could have smuggled contraband blacks into the country to sell them, and still be accepted as a gentleman. Well, accepted by most as a gentleman, but there were those who saw him as a blight on humanity.

The editor smiled slightly to himself. He considered Bowie a compelling sort of man when you came to know him. He had enemies, but he also had friends who seemed quite ready to fight for him. And he made no bones about his record. He admitted the slave-running in a sort of frank, disarming way, without condoning it or excusing it. Something about him made one decide not to hold it against him, any more than one held against other friends the indiscretions of youth, committed before they fully understood their grave implications. But Jim was no youth.

J. Wayne Frye

Jim Bowie: The Vidalia Sandbar Brawl
And the Judalon Affair

Connelly's Tavern, with its two white columns, stood at the edge of the river bluffs and commanded the finest view in Natchez, which was in Mississippi but on the far side of the river was Vidalia, Louisiana and one had a bird's eye view from the front porch of the tavern of the infamous Vidalia Sand Bar. Bold in countenance, Bowie turned over his horse to a black stable boy and went directly to the taproom.

As he reached the door, he could hear a voice expounding medical theories with a sort of obstinate insistence. Bowie opened the door and entered. The voice ceased. It belonged to Dr. Samuel Cuny, a potbellied, self-important little man, addicted to long-winded dissertations in medical jargon. His victim, George McWherters, leaned against the bar, a long-legged man with very blue eyes and curling side whiskers. His expression changed from boredom to relief at Bowie's appearance.

Four other men in the room also turned to look at Bowie. They had been waiting for him. All were members of a business combine.

Bowie saw his brother Rezin sitting across the room where he had been playing cards with Colonel Samuel Wells, a lean, iron-grey man with black eyes set very close together above the bridge of his long bony nose. The colonel's brother, Jefferson Wells, a little less grey and a little less cadaverous, but with the same narrow-eyed family stamp, was simply sitting and watching the game with what appeared disinterest.

Jim Bowie: The Vidalia Sandbar Brawl
And the Judalon Affair

Seated alone, with a glass on the table beside him and a newspaper in his hands, as if he disdained association with the common herd, was General Richard Cuny. The general was imposing, as his brother, the little doctor, was not. His head was very large, with a grizzled frost at the ears and his bearing indicated he took the title of general seriously although he owed his military title to courtesy and custom, rather than to any warlike achievement. He had served a term as attorney general of the state of Louisiana. Not that anybody questioned his personal courage. He had some months before fought a duel with Judge Robert Crain, permanently crippling the judge's left arm with a bullet he had meant for the heart.

The general laid down his newspaper and clambered to his feet with the words "ah, the prodigal returns" directed at Jim.

Many there, along with the general, crowded around Bowie. "Well, what news, Jim?"

Bowie shook his head. "No good."

The general's smile faded. "You mean the bank refused us the loan?"

"That's it."

"But it was as good as approved last week!" said Colonel Wells, his narrow eyes snapping.

Bowie said slowly, "Major Norris Wright bought into the Alexandria bank this week as a stockholder."

They stared. "It was the syndicate's money!" the general exclaimed. "Wright was put there to stop our move. Yes, to stymie our intentions."

J. Wayne Frye

Jim Bowie: The Vidalia Sandbar Brawl
And the Judalon Affair

Dr. Cuny began to swear in a pointless way, damning Major Wright to seven different kinds of hell.

"Shut up, Samuel!" the general said. As if someone had turned him off, the little doctor became silent as the general continued. "Gentlemen, this is grave. We need the twenty-five thousand badly. A heavy, a very heavy disappointment this is indeed. Without that loan I doubt if we can proceed with the transaction." General Cuny pursed his lips, considering gloomily. "It's Judge Crain. That man will never get over hating me for putting my mark on him." He brightened a little; it was a subject he never wearied of discussing. "The ball entered his left arm, but a damn shame I missed the target – his heart."

The others, who had all heard full many a time the details of how the general had wounded the judge, exhibited gloomy concern with the news they had been turned down for the loan.

"As I came up from the landing," Bowie said, "I saw Norris Wright himself with Andrew Marschalk." He paused. "And speaking of Wright, I stopped in at Grady's. The horse is here."

They turned to him quickly at that.

"You've seen him?" Rezin asked.

"Yes. Took time for that."

"How does he look?"

"I saw him by lantern, and we'll have another look in the morning. But I don't think I've ever seen a better horse."

Jim Bowie: The Vidalia Sandbar Brawl
And the Judalon Affair

"If he can win the Duncan Cup, I'd give a thousand for a portrait of Crain's face," the general said.

"Or Wright's," said Rezin. "He thinks that Irish chestnut of his can't be touched."

"The horse has been on a flatboat for days," said Bowie. "The race is Saturday, so he's got only three days to find his legs and his speed. But if what they say is true, and we can get him ready the Alexandria bank loan may not be so important."

They gazed at one another, speculation growing.

"How much?" the general asked.

"Five hundred."

"Share and share. Five hundred into seven portions comes to a little over seventy a piece. Agreed, gentlemen?"

They all nodded affirmatively.

"Since you've made the arrangements, we'll enter him under your name," the general said to Bowie. There were no objections.

"Now, to get a rider," said Jeff Wells.

There, surely, was something to think about and the words came quickly: "My servant, Orlando, can ride," said Major McWherters, tentatively.

Jeff Wells shook his head. "Orlando's too heavy. That boy of Wright's, Juba, is a real jock if he isn't good for anything else, and he's the weight of a tiny female."

Bowie said, "I've got the jockey. I saw Nez Coupé at Alexandria. He's coming up tomorrow. Nez Coupé can ride and handle any animal that eats hay. And he doesn't weigh much more than Juba."

"We can see how he does in the workouts," the general said.

The day of the race, Bowie came down late from his room, arrayed in his best ruffled shirt, burgundy pants and cinnamon coat. He found Rezin and Nez Coupé in the dining room.

"How do you feel?" Bowie said to Nez Coupé.

The Cajun grinned. "Nevair no better."

He had proved to the satisfaction of all the partners his ability as a race rider in secret workouts down a stretch of back country road in the past two days, and he was dressed in his riding boots and scarlet and white silks which Bowie had provided for him.

"How's the horse?"

"Chipper."

"Think he can win?" Bowie grinned.

"By God, Jim, I give that horse ride will open your eyes! Steel Duke, he know me like brother. We make lots of fun, us!"

Nez Coupé, whose confidence in himself was magnificent, rose from the table and swaggered off to see about saddling his horse.

Rezin grinned at Bowie. "Dressed to kill, aren't you?"

"Got to look like somebody today." Bowie grinned back. "I want to look good when I go into the winner's circle."

Between these brothers was great good will. In ten years their family fortunes had made a

Jim Bowie: The Vidalia Sandbar Brawl
And the Judalon Affair

remarkable advance. They owned a plantation in Louisiana; a steam sugar mill at Arcadia, where Rezin lived with his family and his mother; and John, the oldest of the three, had property near Helena, Arkansas, and was being spoken of for the territorial legislature. All of it was due to Jim, the adventurous, imaginative and enterprising man whose name was familiar all over America. Now, however, they were involved in a business crisis, all of them, owing to the refusal of the Bank of Alexandria to make the loan they needed, as Bowie had reported.

"Did old Fraser, the bank president, give any reason for turning us down?" Rezin asked.

"Not the real reason. A lot of bank jargon about collateral and sound principles of finance. He didn't mention that Wright, as a member of the board of directors, had stopped the loan."

"Norris Wright," Rezin mused. "You've got a good enemy there."

"They say a man can be judged by the enemies he makes, and I have made a good one there."

"You've cut him down to size a time or two."

"Well, he thinks he's got us now, like a coon up a tree."

Bowie nodded soberly. The combination confronting the Cuny syndicate, in which the brothers had heavy stakes, was formidable in resources and influence, and actuated by personal feelings, since most of its members had personal vendettas with men in the Cuny faction. Judge Robert A. Crain was General Cuny's bitter foe.

Jim Bowie: The Vidalia Sandbar Brawl
And the Judalon Affair

Major Wright hated Bowie. The brothers, Alfred and Carey Blanchard, related to Judge Crain by marriage, had difficulties with the brothers, Sam and Jefferson Wells. The other member of the Crain group was Dr. Thomas A. Maddox, a sleekly plausible physician, most of whose patients were fashionable women.

The whole financial edifice of the Cuny syndicate was erected like an arch, to which the twenty-five thousand from the bank would have been the keystone. Without the keystone, everything would collapse.

"I'm praying Steel Duke comes through today," said Rezin.

Bowie nodded. "We're betting the pile on him."

At half-past one Bowie and Rezin rode to the track, a half-mile (8/10ths of a kilometre) oval, well levelled and scraped, just outside of the town. Starting time was two o'clock, but already a considerable crowd had gathered, and Rezin went off with some friends, leaving Bowie near the judges' stand.

The lords of the soil, however, who counted their acres by the thousands and their slaves by the score, disdained to rub shoulders with the rabble. Their gleaming carriages paralleled the homestretch in a long line, black grooms at the horses' heads, fashionable loveliness in the upholstered seats, with parasols extended, calling and waving to each other, very animated and bright as the privileged class seem to always be prancing about then and now like peacocks.

Jim Bowie: The Vidalia Sandbar Brawl
And the Judalon Affair

Most of these ladies had been deserted, temporarily, by their escorts, who circulated in a throng near the judges' tower, looking for interesting wagers. Though the Duncan Cup, an ornate silver trophy, was the ostensible prize of the race, much heavier interests would ride with the jockeys this day. Betting had thus far been slow, however, and all odds favoured Major Wright's Irish thoroughbred, Kerry Isle, against the field at four and five to one against any other horse.

The major himself, slim and light-footed, was much in evidence, receiving greetings from his friends, giving laughing assurances to backers, or conversing with a tall, erect man, with iron-gray hair, features well chiselled but cold, and a manner dignified to the point of haughtiness. This was the widely known Judge Crain. Two things about him caught the attention: invariably he dressed in black, and his left arm was in a black silk sling. The sling was a reminder of a certain feud still unsettled in his mind.

Notably aloof from the judge and the major stood Bowie and General Cuny. The general was resplendent in a plum-colour coat with tails hanging almost to his heels. An eye-filling sight was the general. But years exert an unhappy disadvantage, and the younger Bowie was a focus of far greater attention, particularly from the ladies.

Presently Bowie excused himself and walked along the front of the grandstand. His free-and-easy way, his confident bearing made him a favourite with many, but he was disdained by the few, especially the upper crust of society, to many of whom he called by name, not sparing his compliments to their wives, who appreciated the attention of such a virile looking man. Jim did it just to rile the arrogant aristocratic men who thought themselves superior.

Up to this time the supporters of Major Wright's entry had been so confident they posted an offer to take all wagers against their favourite. Few bet, for Kerry Isle was acknowledged as the finest horse in Mississippi and Louisiana, and compared with him the other entries paled. The best of these were Montrose, a black stallion belonging to Colonel Dobson; Baby June, a filly with a rich red gloss, but a trifle light, owned by Boyce Sparling; and Corporal, a big bay with white feet.

Just before starting time the ladies in the carriages noticed a stir of excitement near the judges' stand. Men hurried about or gathered in knots for hurried consultations. Presently to the carriages came a report that there was a last-minute entry. By whom? James Bowie. A horse named Steel Duke. The ladies glanced at each other. None of them had ever heard of Steel Duke, but the fact the horse belonged to Bowie caused a stir. Steel Duke? Where was he from? What kind of a horse was this, and how did he get into this race?

Judge Crain refused to be ruffled, but Major Wright was anxious. The Crain group had

Jim Bowie: The Vidalia Sandbar Brawl
And the Judalon Affair

thousands on this race, and Kerry Isle had been a practical certainty. This might make a difference.

The presiding judge, Andrew Marschalk, stalked over to Bowie. "Where's this horse of yours, sir?"

"He's coming now!"

A little gnome-like man in scarlet and white jockey's silks, with a scarred visage, rode a grey stallion into the enclosure. Every eye watched as Bowie walked over and laid his hand on the horse's polished neck.

Men who prided themselves on knowing horseflesh studied the newcomer and conversed in excited undertones. The animal, it was agreed, looked fast. Vein and muscle made a beautiful tracery under his satin grey skin, his barrel was wonderful, his legs delicate but strong, his head showed blood in every line. Speed without question. Could he match strides for three heats with a horse like Kerry Isle?

A furious Major confronted Bowie. "You smuggled that critter in!" stormed Norris Wright.

Bowie was calm. "Smuggled isn't the word, Major. I bought him. Here in Natchez. And five thousand dollars says he'll beat your horse."

By a prodigious effort Wright controlled his anger. "I've put up with a lot from you, Bowie!" he said in chilled tones. "But this thing tops all the rest. If your trick beats Kerry Isle, big as you are, and regardless of your reputation, look out for yourself!"

All around them heard the threat. Bowie's face did not change. "What about the five thousand?"

J. Wayne Frye

Jim Bowie: The Vidalia Sandbar Brawl
And the Judalon Affair

"I'll lay you the five thousand and another five on top of it!"

"Land, six hundred and forty acres in Rapides Parish, Louisiana"

"Done! I'll match you with a section right next to it!"

Discombobulated by Bowie's cool demeanour, Wright turned and tramped away as the field began filing out onto the track, horses milling about, jockeys curbing them or letting them out for brief bursts of speed down past the grandstand. Wright's jockey, Juba, a little hunchbacked black slave, brought a roar from the crowd as he took Kerry Isle down at a gallop. The Irish thoroughbred was a big raking chestnut with fine shoulders and a prodigious stride, and his was all the advantage in weights. Uncertainty among his supporters, caused by the spectacular arrival of Bowie's horse, disappeared. The chestnut looked a champion if ever a horse did.

Louisiana and Mississippi planters became busy tabulating bets and odds. In the wild excitement money, land, horses, even slaves were wagered. Even out in the long line of carriages, dainty ladies caught the excitement and made quick little notations with jewelled pencils in small leather-covered notebooks; and such is feminine fancy, that many wagered on the gentlemen who owned the horses, rather than on the horses themselves, so that the chestnut carried small bets because of Major Wright's beautiful manners, and the grey because his master was James Bowie.

Jim Bowie: The Vidalia Sandbar Brawl
And the Judalon Affair

A brief consultation at the judges' tower broke up, and Bowie, with Dr. Stephen Duncan, crossed the track. As donor of the race cup he had something to say about the rules.

Bowie, listening to something the doctor was saying, all at once raised his head.

"Isn't that Philippe Cabanal?" he asked with surprise.

"Yes. You know him?"

"Slightly."

Cabanal came up. "Hello, Doctor. It's Bowie, isn't it? How do you do?"

Bowie said, "Very well, thank you. I hadn't heard you were in town."

Not since the night Narcisse de Bornay was killed had he seen Philippe, and he felt in him a curious indefinable change. The man was still well built, well featured, and well dressed, in the world's catalogue a gentleman. But in his face, his nervous vacillating eyes, and his loosened mouth beneath the curling moustache, one who was adept at such things could read signs of weakness, or irresponsibility, perhaps even of pride secretly abandoned.

"We're here on a short visit for business," Philippe said.

"We?"

"Yes. My wife is with me." He looked at Bowie. "You perhaps remember her, Judalon de Bornay?"

Shocked, Jim replied, "I do remember her."

Dr. Duncan said, "In that case, come over to my plantation as Philippe and Judalon are my guests."

Jim Bowie: The Vidalia Sandbar Brawl
And the Judalon Affair

"Certainly," Bowie said, but he felt a stir of misgiving.

Eagerly Philippe turned to the doctor. "What was the discussion?"

"At the judges' stand? It was a question concerning the legality of Mr. Bowie's last-minute entry. But nothing in the rules prevents entries at any time before the race. The only question was the ownership of the horse. A horse entered must belong to the gentleman who enters him, a provision, you understand, to keep out the riffraff. Mr. Bowie avowed his ownership." Dr. Duncan smiled. "Nobody questioned that Mr. Bowie is a gentleman."

Cabanal was worried. "I've got a pretty penny on this race on Kerry Isle. What kind of a horse have you got, Bowie?"

Bowie said, seriously, "I know nothing about him, Philippe. He's fast, and he looks good. But I couldn't tell you to bet on him. You see the odds are on Kerry Isle. I'd gladly tell you if I were sure of the horse or had seen him in a race even once."

"Come, say hello to my wife when you get a chance," Cabanal said and left them.

An increasing trepidation took possession of Bowie. Judalon! The mere mention of her name seemed to bring back to him exactly how she looked ten years ago, how she talked, how she carried her head and smiled. It made him uneasy, this sharpness of recollection, so that he would have preferred to excuse himself from having to converse with her.

Jim Bowie: The Vidalia Sandbar Brawl
And the Judalon Affair

"Perhaps you know that Mrs. Cabanal's mother died?" Dr. Duncan said amiably.

"No. I hadn't heard."

"I mentioned it for fear you might inadvertently bring up a painful subject in the conversation, since you knew her before."

"Thank you for telling me."

There was no avoiding the meeting without discourtesy. They walked toward the row of carriages and he saw Judalon looking at him still beautiful, still stately in every way.

She was in a dress of old gold and blue that melded to her body down to her waist, and then billowed out. She held a small silken parasol tilted over her shoulder. Beside her sat Mrs. Duncan, a somewhat fluttery woman of indeterminate age, who greeted him and began an effusive introduction. Judalon stopped her.

"Mr. Bowie and I are old friends," she said.

"You are?" Mrs. Duncan hesitated, a little confused.

"Very old friends. Aren't we, Jim?" she said as she smiled and held out a gloved hand, tiny as a child's. As he took it, he told himself he had been mistaken. She had changed, but the years had only added to her attraction. Yes, she was more beautiful than ever.

J. Wayne Frye

Jim Bowie: The Vidalia Sandbar Brawl
And the Judalon Affair

Chapter 5
Falling Into Place

"I've just made a wager," Judalon said, "on your horse, a whole hundred dollars. For old times' sake."

He was astonished at his own pleasure that she should have bet on his horse or remembered old times. He was speechless as the horses pulled and fretted at the barrier, swerving out and being swung back into place by their jockeys. The starter, a bull-voiced man with a bald head, cracked a long whip and shouted directions at the top of his lungs. Kerry Isle reared but Steel Duke, behaved well.

A roar from the crowd, and the barrier flew aside. Down the track flashed a riot of silken colours and thundering hoofs. At the first curve and into the backstretch the horses were bunched, but as they passed the grandstand on the first circuit they began to string out, an azure jacket in the lead, Wright's colors. Dobson's lemon and black were close behind. The scarlet and white Nez Coupé wore seemed lost somewhere.

From the crowd a howl of shouts and pleas was hurled across the oval with great excitement.

"Where's that horse of Bowie's?" was heard.

"Can't be found," someone said.

"He's way back!" bellowed someone else.

Kerry Isle's backers lifted their voices to a jubilant scream as she definitely galloped to the lead. Then, in the backstretch, the grey horse seemed to shake his head and lunge forward. He passed Baby June. Corporal faded. Montrose matched strides briefly, then was left behind. Rounding the last curve, Steel Duke's straining nose was within a length of Kerry Isle's tail, but the gap did not close. The grey seemed to have spent himself. Or was the scarlet and white jockey holding him back? Bettors, whose hopes had been raised, bellowed their angry disappointment.

Down the homestretch it was a two-horse race. And Steel Duke was trailing, beaten by a careless ride from its Creole jockey. Then the furious howl of the crowd lifted to a great spontaneous roar, which built and towered as the grey began his drive. Always before, Kerry Isle had taken command in the stretch, but now he found himself unable to shake his rival. Crouched low, his scarlet and white silks whipping in the wind, Nez Coupé for the first time began using the whip while Juba was intensely flogging his mount as the steel-grey head drew forward at the flank, now at the girth, now at the shoulder, now head to head. There they seemed to hang. The wire was in sight as for a moment they thundered nose by nose, heads outstretched. Nez Coupé, lying along his mount's neck, seemed to convey a call for a last burst of speed. The grey responded and under the finish wire he gallantly flashed, a clean winner as the roar of the crowd. Even those who had lost on the race, pounded, applauded and screamed so vociferously that the earth seemed to quiver with excitement at what they had witnessed.

Jim Bowie: The Vidalia Sandbar Brawl
And the Judalon Affair

His scarred face split clear across with his grin Nez Coupé circled the grey stallion past the stand and raised his whip to the judges. A handler gave him a shoulder, and he leaped down from the saddle, so that the horse could be led about, preparatory to sponging him down for the next heat. In her carriage, a woman was exulting, shouting to Jim as he stood by her, "What a beauty! And to think he's yours, Jim!"

Bowie looked up. Judalon was bending toward him, her eyes ablaze, her face beautifully coloured with excitement. She seemed to be espousing his cause. To have a charming woman on one's side is never unpleasant, and he found his old resentment toward her fading fast.

"That first heat was convincing," Dr. Duncan said. "The second may tell the story."

Bowie nodded. He might have gone to the finish wire, but he seemed to be held beside the carriage, trying to understand how he could be so acutely conscious of the woman in it, who had laughed at him once and at a time when a race so important to him was being decided.

Again the kaleidoscope of mingled bright silks whirled by in the roar from the crowd as the second heat began. Judalon rose in the carriage, the parasol tilted behind her head, her body a slender curve of feminine excitement.

"Scarlet and white! He's ahead, no, the chestnut's right behind him! Steel Duke! Steel Duke! Oh, my beauty! Come on, come on, he's running Kerry Isle into the ground! Oh, he's going to win! He's way ahead. It isn't even close! Two lengths at least! He wins! He wins! Oh, what a darling horse you have Jim. No need for a third heat now. 2 out of 3 is a winner indeed."

"Yes," replied Jim, "he is a beauty just like you."

Her eyes went beyond him, and her voice cooled. "Here comes Philippe." Putting animation back in her tone, she called out to him, "I won a hundred, dear!"

"I'm glad somebody won." Philippe's voice was bitter. "I lost. A good bit more than a hundred." Fretfully, he turned on Bowie. "I wish you'd given me that tip I asked for."

"I told you I didn't know myself what he could do."

"You bet on him, didn't you?"

"A man naturally bets on his own horse."

Dr. Duncan said, "If you're interested in selling that horse, I'd like to talk with you. Where did you get him?"

"Bought him only four days ago from a man named Sturdevant."

"Sturdevant?" asked Philippe. "That gambler under the bluff?"

"Yes."

"I know Sturdevant. Where did he get the horse?"

"He told me he won him in a card game from a Nashville man."

"That's interesting. Very interesting," said Philippe.

Jim Bowie: The Vidalia Sandbar Brawl
And the Judalon Affair

Dr. Duncan said, "I'd better return to the judges' stand."

"I'll walk over with you," said Philippe. "Excuse us ladies. Bowie."

Bowie glanced up and found Judalon watching him with a curious gleam of unsmiling interest in her eyes.

"I hope Philippe didn't lose too much," he said.

"I don't know. He's a fool in gambling, and a friend of Major Wright's. You spoke of a man named Sturdevant? He's another of my husband's acquaintances, a very costly one."

Mrs. Duncan said, "There's some kind of excitement at the judges' stand. If I'm not mistaken, they're calling for Mr. Bowie."

He heard his name. "Bowie, Mr. James Bowie please to the judges' stand."

"I wonder what's wrong," he said. "I'd better go."

"Wait," said Judalon. "You must come and see us at the Duncan's plantation."

"Why yes," he offered as he left for the judge's stand.

"Next week? Say Wednesday?"

"I'm sorry. I'm leaving Monday for the north."

"Then this evening. Please Jim and your brother too."

"I'm sure Rezin will be happy. Yes, most certainly we accept, with profound thanks."

He walked away. Judalon's eyes followed him with an odd blending of expressions: admiration, curiosity and speculation. Jim still excited her.

Jim Bowie: The Vidalia Sandbar Brawl
And the Judalon Affair

Troubled faces, angry faces were in the centre of the crowd of men about the judges' stand. Andrew Marschalk, white-thatched and imperturbable, stood listening to a cross fire of questions and resentful exclamations. General Cuny's oratorical visage was dark with wrath. His plump doctor brother puffed and talked in a low voice with Colonel Wells. To one side stood Major Wright, superciliously calm, with Judge Crain and Dr. Maddox. Behind these, hardly a member of the group, as if he observed and listened only, was Philippe Cabanal.

"Why at this time?" Jefferson Wells was demanding of Marschalk.

"May I ask the basis?" insisted Major McWherters.

"I have my opinion, sir, of a protest made after a race is run!" boomed the general. As Bowie came up, General Cuny wheeled on him. "The rules have been invoked, sir, and payment of all wagers held up!"

Bowie took a moment to digest that. "What rule?" he asked.

The dry, precise voice of Andrew Marschalk answered him. "The rule that competing horses shall be the bona fide property of the gentleman entering them must be enforced, sir. Otherwise, what is now a sport in which we all take pride and pleasure would degenerate into shabby thievery."

Very slowly Bowie said, "Does someone here present question the truth of my statement?"

"No, sir. It is a technical point only."

Jim Bowie: The Vidalia Sandbar Brawl
And the Judalon Affair

"I have here a formal bill of sale. Perhaps that will clear up the questions."

Marschalk thanked Bowie, took the paper and read it keenly. After a moment he shook his head. "I fear this instrument only confirms the stewards and judges in their decision."

Every eye turned on Bowie. He spoke in a dangerously quiet voice. "Then I am to understand, sir, that my status as a gentleman is in question?"

"By no means!" Marschalk said quickly. "The character and quality of Mr. James Bowie are most highly regarded by myself and everyone here present, I am most proud to say, sir. Your mere word, unsupported by any paper or other formal proof, would be sufficient. There is no doubt about that."

"Then what are we debating?" interrupted General Cuny. "We hear in one breath an objection that appears to be cleared in the next."

Andrew Marschalk turned to the general, his manner positive, yet courteous. "Neither Mr. Bowie's word or good faith, nor yours, nor those of anyone here are at issue. I assure you, General. What the stewards feel bound to look into are the word and good faith of the man Sturdevant who is a known gambler, a man of the most shady repute, an habitué of the river front to whom more than one crooked transaction and worse has been ascribed."

"I won't attempt to deny that," the general mumbled.

Jim Bowie: The Vidalia Sandbar Brawl
And the Judalon Affair

"The man Sturdevant," continued Marschalk, "asserts, so I am informed, that he won the horse Steel Duke in a card game. This bill of sale bears not only his endorsement, but a signature attributed to one Joseph Levington, of Nashville, Tennessee. I do not know Mr. Levington. Does anyone here know him? I think not. Taking for granted that such a person exists, might not the animal have been stolen from him? Would you undertake to verify this signature, General?"

General Cuny frowned, puffed out his lips, and shook his head. Andrew Marschalk, who in Natchez was above all petty disagreements, had made his position abundantly clear. Though Bowie had paid over the money in good faith, he might not, after all, be the legal owner of the horse. The signature on the bill of sale might very well be forged.

"The decision is difficult," the editor went on. "But very large sums of money and much property are involved. The delay will be, I am sure, a matter of a few days only. I will dispatch a courier to Nashville at once with this paper, to discover Mr. Levington and verify whether or not it is his signature. If all is in order, notice will be given that wagers shall be paid. If not, the wagers shall be paid on the basis that Steel Duke is disqualified and Kerry Isle declared the winner."

Riding back to Connelly's, General Cuny got what comfort he could out of his own conclusions. "Wright knows as well as we do that the title to the horse is perfectly valid," he told Bowie. "He

J. Wayne Frye

raises a technicality which will soon be dissipated. I'd as soon say to his face that, in my bringing up, gentlemen don't hide behind technicalities to avoid paying their losses."

Bowie did not reply. Presently the general chuckled. "The Crain crowd bet their socks on their horse."

Still Bowie was silent.

"Wonder how they learned that we bought Steel Duke from Sturdevant," the general said.

Bowie nodded absently, but he had a different theory. Sturdevant had not been seen at the race. Two other men might have given the information. He remembered his casual conversation with Dr. Duncan and Philippe. But Duncan had raised no question concerning the validity of the horse's ownership, and he was not the kind of man to make such a protest to the judges without notifying Bowie of his intention to do so. Bowie was morally certain that Philippe took the information straight to Major Wright.

A sneaking thing to do, and there was no proof, but it was the kind of thing of which Philippe was capable. Bowie had never liked him. Always he had suspected that Philippe played a role in the fatal quarrel between Narcisse de Bornay and the professional duellist, Contrecourt, the plot having been, of course, to get rid of Bowie himself, in which Narcisse's fatal intervention had not been foreseen. Yet, Judalon, Narcisse's sister, had married Philippe. Surprising how that single fact, which should have had no bearing, clouded and complicated matters, and gave indirection to courses of action which otherwise should have been clearly defined. None of them knew it at the time, but the pieces of a puzzle that would lead to death on the Visalia Sand Bar were falling into place.

Chapter 6
A Bit of Heaven or Hell

The Duncan's plantation was called Auburn, and as Jim and Rezin galloped onto the estate they were aghast at its grandeur, having never been there before. Great white columns, illuminated by hurricane lamps, gleamed a welcome through the trees.

Rezin was silent and troubled. There was something in Jim, there always had been something that aroused in Rezin affection and admiration, not unmixed with pity and even a secret fear for him. Bowie's bluntness and genuineness stemmed from immense inward strength, which was at the same time a source of weakness equally immense.

With a part of the world he was almost irresistible, but he was foreordained, Rezin feared, to be preyed upon always by another part, the subtle, quiet, calculating part of the world, which plays its game with cold and cutting realities. None of the jealousy that sometimes exists even between brothers was in Rezin. He was the elder, but he had long since become the follower of his brother, who was in his mind heroic, like a demigod almost, and yet also like a child, to be humoured, smiled at and watched over.

Jim had broached the matter of the dinner invitation to the Duncan's as soon as they returned to the inn from the race, and added, "Have you met the Cabanals?"

Jim Bowie: The Vidalia Sandbar Brawl
And the Judalon Affair

"Yes," Rezin said. "A day or two before you returned from Alexandria."

"What did you think of them?"

"Of Cabanal, that he is a nobody. Of Mrs. Cabanal, that she's remarkably beautiful."

"Anything else?"

"I think remarkably intelligent."

"Nothing more?"

"Perhaps selfish and calculating."

Jim said, "Why does everyone suspect that of a woman merely because she has beauty?"

"Because a beautiful woman is hard to understand, I reckon. Homeliness seems always to clarify a woman's nature, because it appears to have been produced by the weaknesses and virtues of the spirit under it. But beauty gives a woman mystery, because you're damned well sure her spirit's got nothing to do with her looks. She might very likely be the exact opposite of what she seems to be."

After a little silence, Rezin reflectively said, "This is the girl in whom you were interested in New Orleans?"

He took Jim's silence for assent.

"Did your previous experience give you a different impression of her?"

Bowie said slowly, "How can I judge when I don't know the full story?"

When they dismounted and entered the great house, they perceived that the company was numerous. "It's more of an affair than I thought," Jim said.

J. Wayne Frye

Jim Bowie: The Vidalia Sandbar Brawl
And the Judalon Affair

Rezin stopped at the entrance to the reception room. "I take it we got a last-minute invitation," he said under his breath. "The whole Crain crowd's here."

It was true. But in spite of that, Jim looked at the scene with a momentary pleasure. Under these conditions women always were at their best. They reminded him of a cloud of butterflies in the brilliant candlelight.

Individuals began to catch his eye. The tall Blanchard brothers conversed with a pair of pleasant Natchez matrons. Philippe Cabanal stood laughing with Mrs. Duncan. Beyond was Dr. Maddox, talking to the angular daughter of Colonel Dobson, with his careful manners so nicely calculated to impress susceptible women. Major Wright, however, seemed somewhat bored by his partner, a rustic maiden from one of the back plantations, all fluffy curls and flashing teeth, who simpered so adoringly at him that his pain was obvious. On the far side of the room stood Judge Crain, in black as usual, chatting in a courtly manner with Judalon.

"The judge always wears that sling," observed Jim to Rezin.

"Not to be ill-natured," Rezin said, "I don't think he needs it. I'm reliably informed that the arm's healed, a little stiff, maybe, but well enough. But the judge isn't one to miss a chance to be conspicuous. That sling, I've no doubt, will be a mark of his personal appearance the rest of his life."

Jim Bowie: The Vidalia Sandbar Brawl
And the Judalon Affair

Mrs. Duncan bore down upon them. She asked Rezin to take in Miss Fulton of Fair Oaks in to dinner. And would James be so good as to conduct Mrs. Cabanal?

The gentlemen were enchanted, but Judalon turned and smiled into Jim's eyes. Almost numbingly he felt her old spell beginning to reassert itself over him.

Beside them Major Wright halted with a little bow. "Miss Judalon, your servant. Mr. Bowie."

"Oh, hello, Norris," said Judalon casually.

Bowie stiffened. "Major Wright."

Visibly the two men measured each other. Judalon surveyed them with a little dancing light in her eyes.

"You gentlemen are acquainted, I take it?"

A quick gleam came upon Major Wright. "Yes. We hunt in the same country."

"Together?"

"No. Mr. Bowie runs with his own pack of hounds," Wright replied in a sarcastic tone.

The dining room was large. Forty sat down that evening to a wonderful banquet, but Jim hardly knew what he was eating, and the jests and laughter and compliments which passed across the table left him out, for he was almost completely occupied with Judalon.

At the far end of the table Major Wright sat stiffly with the belle from the remote plantation. It amused Judalon, who called Bowie's attention to it. Across the table, Rezin was conducting, as well as he could, a conversation with a middle-aged

J. Wayne Frye

Jim Bowie: The Vidalia Sandbar Brawl
And the Judalon Affair

spinster whose chief interest in life was the harp. His attention wandered. He found himself studying Judalon: trying to read her with great scrutiny as she toyed with Jim.

She said to Rezin, "I was just telling Jim what a surprise it was to meet him here."

Rezin smiled. "Jim's full of surprises."

Dinner ended. Some of the guests were dancing in the ballroom to a piano. Others played in the card room. A few engaged in conversation in the drawing room. With one or two other men, Bowie and Rezin smoked in the library with Dr. Duncan.

Presently, in a low voice, Rezin said to Jim, "I saw you talking to the major. What did he have to offer?"

"Nothing worth mentioning."

"You know he's jealous of you, don't you?"

"Why?"

"Judalon."

To Jim, it was ridiculous. He threw his cigar into the grate and left the library. Judalon was in the ballroom. When she saw Jim, she straightened at once and came over to him.

Bowie saw Wright's eyes follow her. Perhaps the man was jealous.

He said, "You aren't playing the piano?"

"No. You promised me something."

"What was it?"

"To tell me what you've been doing. Let's go in here," she said as she led him into the solarium.

He attempted to tease her. "Your husband may not like this."

J. Wayne Frye   115

She gave him a gleaming smile. "Do you care?" "No."

The implications were stunning. She said, "Philippe does not love me, as I have good reason to know."

They were completely alone. He leaned toward her. "Judalon," he whispered.

She allowed him to kiss her.

Then she indignantly said, "What, oh, what have you done?" With a wild and untranslatable look at him, she fled.

For five minutes Bowie sat alone in the solarium. Never in all his life had he been so shaken by a woman. She had led him on twice now and ingloriously plunged a dagger of emotion into his heart. "Damnable woman," he thought.

When he rose after a time the muscles of his legs were still quivering. Rezin was in the library, deep in bookish talk with Dr. Duncan. Bowie did not summon him. He found Mrs. Duncan and made his farewells.

The trees made a dark canopy, shutting out the moonlight as he rode alone from the Duncan's. He rode in profound abstraction. As lasting as a bee sting, the warm sensation of Judalon's lips remained with him. Convention called for fury from a woman kissed against her will, but she had willingly consented by her actions if not by words.

Perhaps, he contemplated; he had done her the terrible injustice by misjudging her intentions. He found her beautiful, wonderful, and did she not show genuine interest?

Jim Bowie: The Vidalia Sandbar Brawl
And the Judalon Affair

Still, Judalon was married. His mind told him this was an impenetrable obstacle. Yet, all the time he thought of her off and on for ten years now. He had never put her out of his mind.

Approaching the end of the tree-shadowed avenue, he sensed, rather than saw, his horse's head lift at a sound which seconds later his own ears distinguished, the unmistakable cadence of a galloping horse.

It brought him out of his abstraction. He firmed his reins and pressed his knees on the horse's sides. The animal broke into a canter. The trees thinned ahead, and he rode out on the wide turnpike, clear and bright in the moonlight.

"Bowie!" hailed someone.

He knew the voice: Major Norris Wright. "Sir! I want a word with you!"

Bowie stopped.

Wright said, "I've watched you this evening, Bowie. Your actions are offensive, sir. You will leave Mrs. Cabanal alone in the future. Do you understand that?"

"On your say-so, Wright, I understand no such thing."

"Philippe Cabanal is my good friend. And I admire Judalon Cabanal. You, sir, owe them both an apology!"

"I don't consider that I need to explain to you, sir, or apologize to anyone!"

"I warn you let her alone!"

"You're pretty free with your warnings, Major. Suppose you let Philippe or Judalon tell me."

Jim Bowie: The Vidalia Sandbar Brawl
And the Judalon Affair

"That's your answer?"

"Yes."

"Then you'll answer to me now!" Wright's voice was choked.

Bowie saw the pistol in the darkness. The flash of it firing lit the ground, the trees and the faces of both men for one quivering instant. With the heavy shock of the report in his ears, Bowie felt a jolt at his side, a numbing but no pain.

Jim's horse began to plunge, wild with fright. Rage seemed to dim the moonlit scene with a reddish hue as Bowie controlled the horse and circled back.

Staring as if he could not believe, Wright sat motionless in his saddle. "I couldn't have missed."

Bowie's horse swung close. "You had no call to fire on me, Wright!"

Jim's own pistol was in his hand. Wright did not stir as Bowie thrust the weapon forward cocking it in the process. The hammer clicked, but there was no report, no spurt of flame. It was a misfire.

Bowie hurled the pistol to the ground, and his horse, spurred and reined sidewise, cannoned into the major's mount, almost knocking it off its feet. At the same moment he grappled for Wright.

One powerful hand seized the major by the shoulder, another closed on his elbow. Wright struggled, dashing his bleeding fist again and again into his enemy's face. Rising in his stirrups, Bowie lifted the other out of his saddle. Together they tumbled headlong to the ground. A snarling, brutal struggle ensued.

Jim Bowie: The Vidalia Sandbar Brawl
And the Judalon Affair

A shout, a pounding of hoofs could suddenly be heard. Other guests leaving the plantation had heard Wright's shot. Men rode out of the avenue's blackness, leaped from horses, dragged Bowie from the major's struggling body.

"Jim! Jim!" Rezin pleaded.

"He fired on me without warning," Bowie said thickly.

"Come away. Nothing you can do now in haste," offered Rezin.

Almost stumbling to his horse, he mounted and rode off with Rezin. Norris Wright stood in a group of his friends, feeling his throat, his pallid hatred clear in the moonlight.

Bowie, stripped to his waist, stood in Rezin's room at Connelly's. Dr. Cuny stooped over, squinting professionally at his naked side. Just above the waistline a purpling, angry bruise swelled; a bruise fresh and painful, shot with little blood streaks, but after all, only a bruise.

"No doubt of it, the bullet struck here," said Dr. Cuny. "But no penetration fortunately." Then, he continued. "This is something that can't be passed over, James. You've got to challenge!"

"I don't know." Bowie seemed to be inwardly debating. "If it's anyone's move, I think it's Wright's."

"Preposterous, sir! Under the code you have every warrant. Unprovoked and treacherous attack, vilification and abuse. It demands action!"

"As to the assault, I reckon Wright's throttle is going to be mighty tender with the finger marks I left on his neck," said Bowie slowly. "We'll say that things, so far, are about even."

"Do you deny that Major Wright deserves killing?"

The general drew himself up somewhat coldly. "I congratulate you, sir, on having suffered no very serious hurt. Now, since it's late and we all need sleep, my brother and I will retire."

Bowie put on his shirt when the Cuny's were gone.

"You think I ought to send a challenge, too?" he asked Rezin.

"No."

"Thanks."

"But I'm afraid you're going to have to come to conclusions with Norris Wright, sooner or later."

"I reckon."

It was this night that made Jim Bowie contemplate that guns had drawbacks, but a knife, as he had proven in the battle against Contrecourt was more reliable. He weighed his knife in his hand. The hilt gave it an awkward balance, the weight up against the handle. No good for throwing. Still, the beginnings of an idea came to him, an idea that had been lying fallow for years. When he was a long-legged youth, he had played at throwing knives with the Cajun boys and achieved a fair skill at it. A knife, to be a good weapon, should be throwable. He said, "Thanks, Rezin," and tossed the knife on the bed. On his face was an absent calm as he put on his waistcoat, with the ragged bullet hole in the pocket, and then his coat. At this moment Rezin felt he knew what was on his brother's mind.

Sure enough, it came out. Bowie asked, "What did you think of her?"

He took it for granted that there was only one "her" worthy of notice at the Duncan's that night. Rezin did not equivocate. "She's married, Jim."

Jim nodded slowly. "I won't see her again. I'm leaving for Little Rock in the morning, instead of waiting for Monday. By the way, "Who's the best blacksmith you know?"

Rezin was surprised at the abrupt change in subject. "Why let's see. There's John Sowell, right here in Natchez. A good man. And Snowden at Opelousas. And what's the matter with Jesse Cliffe at Arcadia?"

"I want somebody who knows all there is to know about steel."

Rezin pondered. "John was telling me about some Arkansas man, last time he was home. Said he knew more about steel than anyone. Let me see the name is Black. Has a shop at Washington."

"I reckon I'll pay a visit to Washington, Arkansas on my way north."

"Out of your way a considerable piece. Must be important."

"One of the most important things I have ever done, brother."

Rezin was too greatly relieved at finding his brother putting the New Orleans woman out of his mind to argue either for more information or against the long detour.

Jim Bowie: The Vidalia Sandbar Brawl
And the Judalon Affair

It was a long journey from Natchez, and Bowie and Nez Coupé, his companion who by now had been truly declared the winner of the Duncan Cup had a sufficiency of salt meat and noisy taverns by the time they reached Washington. They were pleasantly surprised; however, to find that the town was no log-cabin village, that its homes and commercial buildings were well constructed, and that Elijah Stuart's inn possessed clean beds and a decent table.

When they ate supper, Stuart, a big man with a genial manner, sat at the table with them.

"Know of a smith by the name of Black in these parts?" Bowie asked.

Stuart allowed that, yes, there was a shop owned by James Black, right up Franklin Street at the edge of town and that he was so good at his trade that he kept five slaves busy meeting the demand for his product.

Early the following morning Bowie found the shop, a big shed with double doors through which a wagon could be run, a tall brick chimney at the back, and a sign in front which read: *JAMES BLACK - SMITHING AND CUTLERY*.

He entered the place and what caught Bowie's attention was a great blast furnace at the back, like a brick kiln in appearance, something not often seen in blacksmith shops. A slave, naked to the waist, came up respectfully. "Mr. Black?" Bowie asked above the clangour at the anvils.

The slave nodded. His black arm extended as he pointed toward the office.

J. Wayne Frye

Jim Bowie: The Vidalia Sandbar Brawl
And the Judalon Affair

Bowie went in, closing the door behind him to shut out part of the noise. From behind a desk a thin, nervous man, with dark hazel eyes, long black hair brushed back behind his ears, and a forehead greatly wrinkled gazed keenly at him.

"Mr. Black? My name is Bowie. I've been informed that you make a good cutting edge."

"I make a try at it, sir."

"You have a different tempering method?"

"So they say."

"In what respect?"

Black's face chilled. "By your leave, sir, that's a trade secret."

"I only asked because I have a special job. A kind of knife I want made."

The smith was interested. "I was a cutler before I came west from Philadelphia. Fine knives are a sort of hobby with me, but we don't have much call for them here."

Bowie held out a piece of carved wood. "I sort of whittled this out," he explained.

Black nodded. It was customary for men to bring whittled models, since the draftsman's art was almost unknown on the frontier. In long, nervous fingers, he took Bowie's piece of carved white pine and turned it over and over.

"Some novel features in this idea," he said.

"Just a rough beginning of what I mean," said Bowie. From the sheath at his belt he drew his knife and handed it to Black. "This thing has killed, but it lacks character. It is not really for fighting."

Jim Bowie: The Vidalia Sandbar Brawl
And the Judalon Affair

In one hand Black held Jim's knife and in the other the wooden model. The superior formation of the latter was evident.

"These are the proportions you want?" he asked.

"Roughly, but I shall accede to your superior knowledge."

Black returned the knife and, taking up a rule, made a series of measurements on the carved pattern.

"Blade, eleven inches long (28 centremetres), and an inch and a half wide (4 centremetres)," he said.

"That can vary a little, according to the balance."

"The heel at the back seems exceptionally thick. I get three eighths of an inch (7.5 centremetres) here."

"That's to give it strength. Above all, it must not snap."

The smith nodded. Bowie took the pattern and began to outline some of its features, very carefully. "Observe this: the point is to come at the exact centre of the width of the blade. That's to give it accuracy in throwing. Nothing worse than an off-center point when you try to stick a knife in a target. Furthermore, it provides a certain balance which you will appreciate."

Black's eyes gleamed as he nodded again.

"The blade curves to the point convexly from the edge, and concavely from the back," said Bowie. "Both those curves must be as sharp as the edge of the blade itself."

J. Wayne Frye

Jim Bowie: The Vidalia Sandbar Brawl
And the Judalon Affair

"I can see that. An excellent feature. Particularly since you want the blade so thick."

"The cross guard is very important. It should be of heavy brass instead of steel. Also, I want a backing of brass along the heel of the blade, running to where the curve toward the point begins."

"Why brass, Mr. Bowie?"

"Brass is softer than steel. It will catch a cutting edge. In parrying a thrust, the other blade won't slip off so easy."

"Very clear. Very logical."

"The rest of it is naturally up to you, if you want to undertake it." Bowie handed back the model. "The knife must be balanced so it can be thrown. You'll arrive at that when you know the weight of the blade in relation to hilt and handle."

Black nodded. "Of course. A nice problem there."

"There's something else that I'm not wholly sure is possible, but I want to give it to you as a notion." Bowie hesitated.

"Very well."

"I was once shown a weapon, a kind of sword it was, used by fighting men in the Middle Ages, when they had to cut at steel armour. It had a feature that's always interested me. I've thought it over a good many times since. A weight, called a steel apple, slid in a groove along the back of the blade toward the point when a blow was struck. It put something extra into the swing, an added power. Naturally a steel apple wouldn't be

Jim Bowie: The Vidalia Sandbar Brawl
And the Judalon Affair

practical in a knife, but if you gather what I mean, a weighting of the blade, maybe toward the point to give a shrewder stroke. I'll leave that with you for what it's worth."

Black took a long time thinking this over. "It would take study," he said at length. "As for the steel, it will be the best I can make, and that's as good as you can get. You've heard of Damascus steel?"

"Yes, sir."

"The world never saw steel that would take and keep an edge like Damascus, or was as springy, yet strong. It had a peculiar mottling due to the process of its making. Would it surprise you to know that I make steel with such mottling, perhaps the true Damascus?"

"Indeed, yes," Bowie said.

"I'm not sure it's exactly the same. I discovered the process by an accident. But I'm certain it's the best steel that can be produced by the methods we have today, and yet, it's possible to make better. Let me show you something."

From a drawer of his desk he took a wooden box, brassbound and locked. With a key taken out of his pocket he unlocked it. Within, on velvet lay an object, dark and irregularly round, half the size of a man's fist. He lifted it out.

"Take it," he said.

In Bowie's hand it was surprisingly heavy. "What is it?"

"Steel. Pure steel. And of a quality never made on this earth."

Jim Bowie: The Vidalia Sandbar Brawl
And the Judalon Affair

"Then how?"

"Let me recite an experience. As a boy, working on a farm in Pennsylvania, I saw a fireball pass across the sky so bright that it made even the sun seem secondary for a moment, leaving a trail of incandescent bellowing smoke behind it. When it disappeared over the horizon, terrific thunderclaps were heard, and weird sounds which I can only liken to the bellow of oxen, the roar of a fire in a chimney and the tearing of cloth. This was followed by a detonation like a tremendous explosion. It was the death of a meteor."

He paused, his keen intellectual face showing the impression made on him by the heavenly visitation. "It terrified the countryside. Many thought it presaged the end of the world. But it started me on a career. I went to the place where fragments of the meteor fell and discovered some pieces, of which, this was the largest. Later I learned something remarkable about this piece."

"What was that?"

"Some meteorites are chiefly stone. Others are chiefly iron, smelted in the heavenly furnace of their own heat as they enter the earth's atmosphere. But this is steel, genuine steel produced by some process which must have included passage in superheated form through atmospheric ice. Its hardness is such that it is almost impossible to cut it, even with a diamond. These things occur but rarely in meteorites, yet here it is, and I have waited, waited patiently for the right smithing job to use it."

J. Wayne Frye 127

Jim Bowie: The Vidalia Sandbar Brawl
And the Judalon Affair

He then stared intently at Jim. I know the name Bowie. I know your reputation with a knife. I know of the night, when in a locked room you went up against a skilled swordsman and bested him. "Mr. Bowie, I have been waiting for a man like you to make a one of a kind knife, one of a kind like no other in this world. In fact, it shall be a knife forged out of materials from another world.

Bowie had listened with deep interest. "I believe I've brought my knife idea to the right man."

"Thank you, sir." Black nodded. "You've given me something different to work on, something which greatly intrigues me. Come back in a month. We'll see what can be accomplished."

Was this story true about forging a knife from fragments of a meteorite? There is no way to verify the story's veracity, only reiterate the facts presented from many sources and lay them bare before the reader who can come to his or her own conclusion. After all, Jim Bowie is both man and legend!

For the month Bowie was gone, James Black sat at his desk turning over in his fingers the whittled wooden pattern. To every part of his nature the problem of the knife appealed. His eyes took in each contour of the blade. Clearly a product of thinking, as well as of instinctive judgment of the knife as a weapon, with each minute that he studied the carved model his respect for the man who had brought it to him grew. To make a knife in this shape was easy, but to give it all the hidden

J. Wayne Frye

qualities Bowie had suggested would be immeasurably difficult. James Black slept fitfully night after night. He was in the tug of an immense inspiration, the pull of an idea.

As time passed, Black felt that the elements of his steel had sintered into something of sufficient perfection. It was the blade itself that brought the real gleam to his eye. This was no ordinary knife, no thin polished slip of steel likely to snap like glass or bend at too great a strain. It was as if two or three ordinary knives had been welded together, the backbone powerful. In curve from spine to point, and in curve from edge to point, there was a harmony deeply satisfying. He tested the edge with a wetted thumb. No razor could be more sinisterly keen.

Then Jim walked into the shop and gazed upon the weapon in awe. He took the knife and twanged it with his thumb. From it came a clear, bell-like sound.

"Try throwing it. That board yonder."

The knife sang through the air, struck and gave a high vibrant note as it quivered in its target. Bowie walked over and drew it from the plank. He looked at the cold bluish lustre of the blade. It was something like ice. He put it to his tongue. It tasted bitter and raw like the sea. He sniffed at it. It smelt like blood. "I never thought such a knife could be," he marvelled. "What did you do to make it, James Black?"

"Something that can hardly be done again," said Black, his voice almost mystical. "I fused into it a fragment of a star. For better or for worse, this knife of yours has a bit of heaven in it or a bit of hell."

Fact or fiction? Was Bowie's knife really forged from a meteorite?

Jim Bowie: The Vidalia Sandbar Brawl
And the Judalon Affair

Chapter 7
He Would Be Wrong

Nez Coupé was ecstatic. He spent half an hour lovingly considering the knife's keenness. As they bedded down for the night, he stepped to an oak tree and tried it. A thick branch was sheared through like a melon, and his thumb on the edge found no diminution of the razor keenness. Truly this was a blade beyond all blades. He gazed at Bowie. "This knife, she is death."

Bowie nodded and took it back, as if he begrudged the time it was in the other's possession. Its mere weight in his hands gave him a sense of power and confidence. His new, strange, miraculously keen weapon was as a fulfillment of his nature. His life seemed to focus on it and its hilt in the sheath on his hip gave him a harsh joy. The thing almost went to his head. James Black had spoken of something added, a bit of heaven, or perhaps of hell. Bowie was not far from attributing supernatural properties to his knife. It was as ever bit as beautiful as Judalon, and even deadlier.

At Monroe, Louisiana, he and Nez Coupé parted, for the Cajun had to take the road west to Arcadia. Bowie continued to Natchez. He found that Rezin, who had been home in the interim, had returned to Connelly's tavern to await him. "Andrew Marschalk's courier got back from Nashville the week after you went north," he said.

Bowie looked up.

Jim Bowie: The Vidalia Sandbar Brawl
And the Judalon Affair

Rezin had good news as he cheerfully said to Jim, "Most of the bets from the race have been paid."

"What about Wright's?" asked Jim.

"Wright hasn't made a settlement for what he owes you yet, but I'm persuaded that he will."

"I want that five thousand and that cotton farm," said Bowie.

Rezin nodded. "You've been away. Give him time. Whatever Wright is, he's no liar." He grinned. "I hear Judge Crain had to sell property to settle his obligations. It didn't set well with him or with the others. They've done a lot of complaining over at the tavern."

"Along what lines?"

"For one thing, they're now saying that Joseph Levington of Nashville, while of good family, is prone to lose his judgment when in drink. On the night in question, he was so drunk, so they say, that he didn't know one card from another, and so was bled by Sturdevant. Some of his friends next day urged him to revoke his bet, but Levington signed the bill of sale when it was presented."

"He should have. It was a debt of honour."

"The tavern crowd has tried to infer that the incident, to say the best for it, was irregular."

"Gives them some satisfaction, I suppose."

"When you left town so early next morning after the quarrel with Wright, there was a little talk. Your return will put a stop to that, and I think Wright himself never suspected you of running away. Wright's had time to cool off."

Jim Bowie: The Vidalia Sandbar Brawl
And the Judalon Affair

"Don't bet on that," growled Jim.

To himself Rezin conceded it would be a poor wager. That day in Natchez, sporting bloods were making and taking bets as to whether his brother or Norris Wright would send the challenge, and which of them would die. It was taken for granted that one or the other of the two was living on borrowed time. We've had a fracas since you left. Know Montfort Wells of Alexandria?"

Bowie did. Montfort Wells was an older brother of Colonel Sam Wells, an aging man, somewhat palsied and squinting through thick glasses, since his sight was dimmed by cataracts in both eyes.

"It appears that Dr. Maddox of the Crain party circulated a yarn about old Montfort. Its exact nature I've not been able to learn, since Colonel Wells, naturally, is reluctant to discuss it. But I gather it is of a scandalous nature involving a woman."

Jim grinned and offered the opinion that the type of scandal alleged might have been taken as a compliment, considering the years and fading manhood of the elder Wells.

Rezin grinned back. "Old Montfort is past seventy and has palsy, he sent a note to Maddox demanding the source of the story. Maddox refused to state anything beyond the fact that it came from a lady patient of his. Yesterday, while in Alexandria on business, he encountered old Montfort, who stepped into his office, fetched out a double-barrelled shotgun, and pulled both triggers. His shooting was deplorable. He can hardly make out a moving figure at ten paces, you know. The charge merely truncated the doctor's coattails and bagged a mule beyond. The animal, which was drawing a cotton cart, overturned the cart and injured the field hand who was driving it. Montfort was deeply mortified because the mule, the darkie and cart belonged to a friend of his. Of course he insisted on paying damages. Maddox returned somewhat hastily to Natchez."

Jim laughed.

"By the way," Rezin went on, "will you dispose of your share in Steel Duke?"

"Dr. Duncan?"

"Yes. Five thousand dollars is the offer. A clean ten-for-one profit. The others all want to sell."

Bowie nodded. "Dr. Duncan spoke to me about it. I wouldn't stand in the way of the others."

"Speaking of Duncan," said Rezin, "reminds me that your friends are still there at Duncan's plantation."

"The Cabanals?"

"Yes, Judalon is still here. A rather lengthy visit, I'd say."

"The Duncan's are most hospitable. And I think Mrs. Duncan and Judalon are very fond of each other."

"Saw Judalon recently in town. She inquired about you." Rezin paused. "Major Wright's been out to the Duncan's a lot since you left."

"How often?" Jim asked.

"Couldn't say, since I don't keep tabs either on Wright or the Duncan plantation. But I'd say over

Jim Bowie: The Vidalia Sandbar Brawl
And the Judalon Affair

there often. Some of the ladies in the town are beginning to gossip about it, and so it gets to the men, and that's how it came to me. They're saying that Wright's sweet on Judalon."

"What about Philippe?"

"Don't know. You'd wonder, naturally, why he'd ever stand for it. He knows about it, surely. Maybe it's all aboveboard. You know how gossip distorts things. In any case, he and Wright are together a good part of the time when he's in town. He's been doing a lot of gambling at King's tavern, and, I'm informed, down under the bluff also."

It was a subject Bowie was willing to drop. The Duncan's were respectable. Certainly they knew what was proper and what was not. On the other hand, they were the sort who would never interfere in the affairs of others and would keep their opinions to themselves when guests in their home were involved.

Jim went to his room, an ugly feeling in him. Judalon had taken Bowie's kiss, and her marriage had not stood in the way of it. Why not another man's?

In the illogical way of the jealous, he grew angry toward the woman; already condemning her in his mind. No telling what had been going on since he went north. The image of her had remained in his heart and the taste of her on his mouth, a lasting mischief of his libido.

Always he had been mystified by the strange exaltation, naturalness, even innocence of women

Jim Bowie: The Vidalia Sandbar Brawl
And the Judalon Affair

once they resolved to abandon the familiar cloaking of custom and behaviour. Judalon, however, was not to be put in any category, because there was no understanding her.

What was Norris Wright to her? An ugly rage, an endless dislike of the sleek major burned in him. Wright had tried to kill him. This was something that must be settled between them. He made up his mind that he would call out Major Norris Wright.

He considered the matter and fondled the knife in its sheath on his hip. But this would be no affair of knives. Without any question the major would choose pistols.

Next morning a young black boy on a long-legged colt brought a note to Connelly's Inn where Jim was staying while in town. The note was simple and direct: *Mr. James Bowie: The undersigned prays that you come to the Duncan Plantation, if convenient for you, at 3 P.M. this day on a matter which she is persuaded is of importance to you. Please answer by messenger. Faithfully, Judalon de Bornay Cabanal.*

Bowie considered the matter for a moment, scribbled a note of acceptance, and gave it to the boy, along with a half dollar.

He ate lunch with Rezin, saying nothing of Judalon's note, and when his brother, who had business in the cotton exchange, left him he went to the upper gallery of the inn to sit alone.

Connelly's commanded an unsurpassed view. In a mighty curve the river swept below him, the

Jim Bowie: The Vidalia Sandbar Brawl
And the Judalon Affair

tree-dotted plain of Louisiana beyond with the distant buildings of Vidalia, and the low-lying Vidalia Sandbar Island, green and wooded, was near the far shore.

The man he least expected to see came out on the gallery and looked at him. Philippe Cabanal hurried over and offered his hand. "Just heard you were back, Bowie. Been gone a long time, haven't you? We've missed you."

Such friendliness was neither timely nor required. Bowie said coldly, "How are you, Philippe?"

"Well enough, I suppose. They told me you were up here. I took the liberty of coming up. Dr. Duncan, who'd been in town, brought word last night that you'd returned from the north. Judalon was as delighted as am I. I wanted to talk with you alone. There's a personal thing. What I want to discuss is the matter of a loan."

"A loan?"

"Well," Philippe said, "that's the awkward part of it. I went a bit over my head in the Duncan Cup. Who'd have dreamed you'd bring in that animal of yours?"

Bowie said, "You can't pay your losses?"

"To put it short, that's exactly it."

"Let me understand this. I was under the impression that you had more than enough with your father's estate and your wife's to settle any debt."

Philippe looked down at the floor. "It's unpleasant to discuss personal affairs, but I'll give you an explanation in confidence you understand. My own money is gone because of unfortunate business investments. Could happen to anybody. So we're living on Judalon's income."

"I see."

"Unhappily, her mother left it so that she gets it in quarterly instalments which is not enough to meet our obligations. I'd hoped to recoup a little on that horse race. Instead, I'm deeper in than ever."

Bowie was silent.

Philippe gave him an odd look. "You had a wager with Major Wright."

"I did."

"Perhaps you're wondering why it's not been paid?"

"I suppose."

"He gave me the money and the deed to bring over. I took the liberty of holding it because, as you say, you were away."

"That was quite a liberty, Philippe."

"Don't be angry, I beg of you. You've no idea the trouble I'm in."

"You have the payment here?"

"The deed to the land." Philippe drew from a pocket the folded document.

For a moment Bowie glanced it over to see that it was in proper form. Then he looked up. "There was also five thousand in cash."

"That is what I want to bring up. About that money, I'm going to make a request that I hope you'll find feasible."

Jim Bowie: The Vidalia Sandbar Brawl
And the Judalon Affair

"You don't have it?"

"It happens that I overextended myself by just about that amount. Permit me to keep the five thousand say for ninety days, won't you? It would pull me out of a bad hole. Maybe you could do it for Judalon's sake.

"What does she have to do with it?"

"Nothing, but I know you think a lot of her, don't you? Always have. It would be a terrible humiliation to my wife if I were denounced. Much worse for her than for me. Don't you think?"

"Does Judalon know?" Bowie asked.

"Not a thing."

"Let it go as a loan then."

Philippe departed, but paused at the door with his smile. "Don't forget. You are welcome at the Duncan's. I'm sure Judalon will be eager to see you any time."

What a deplorable cad thought Jim. Still, Judalon held a great fascination with Jim. Thus he gleefully trotted his horse down the shaded Duncan drive, left the animal with a stable boy, and went up the steps.

"Mrs. Cabanal?" he said to the servant who opened the door.

"This way, suh." He was conducted to the drawing room.

Judalon was alone. She rose. "You're prompt. Thank you for coming," she said. "We are alone and can talk for a minute without interruption. Come over here by the window and sit down, won't you?"

Jim Bowie: The Vidalia Sandbar Brawl
And the Judalon Affair

"You'll want to know why I asked you to come here."

"Yes. I am a little curious," he replied.

"The reason was personal. I took the earliest opportunity of communicating with you, because of the pressing nature of the matter."

"It must be important."

She regarded him seriously. "Since you got back, have you met Major Wright?"

"No."

"I want you to promise me you'll let it go no farther."

"I didn't make that quarrel," he said.

"But you can avoid further aggravation of it."

"You really think it's as simple as that?"

"Why should men be enemies? At least promise me that you will not send the challenge. If it comes, let it come from him. Will you promise that, Jim?"

"Why are you worrying over Norris Wright? And why are asking this of me rather than of him?" he demanded.

Her mood underwent one of its lightning changes. All at once she was soft and sweet. "Because I know your kindness, Jim, and your common sense, and I thought you'd grant me something I earnestly desire."

"I'll promise that if there's a challenge it won't come from me."

Her face brightened. "You make me happy, very happy. I only wish I could say the same of Philippe, but alas I can't. I know men have

Jim Bowie: The Vidalia Sandbar Brawl
And the Judalon Affair

mistresses. It is winked at; women prefer security to scandal and therefore suffer in solitude. But this is the finish. As surely as you and I are sitting here, I am going to free myself from that man. Jim, I need your friendship. Divorce is such a dreadful thing. I'm afraid."

She seized his hand in both her own and clung to it. Immense emotion surged through him. "Don't be afraid," he whispered. "When you're free Judalon, will you marry me?"

"You'd do that for me?" she asked.

"Yes."

She put his hand against her breast, and he could feel her heart beating upon it. She drew a little breath. Then she withdrew her hands and said, "Thank you for that."

Some things are beyond the power of flesh and blood to withstand. He groped for her. The memory of her lips intoxicated him. He hungered to feel them again. She put out her arms and held him back. There was to be no kiss this time. Jim got up and said goodbye reluctantly.

When Bowie reached the end of the Auburn lane, he saw a horseman galloping down the turnpike toward him from Natchez. It was Philippe. He brought his horse to a jolting stop.

"You've seen Judalon?"

"Yes."

"Sorry to have missed you."

He lifted his reins, but pulled up his horse again after the animal had begun to move. "Hear what happened?" he asked.

Jim Bowie: The Vidalia Sandbar Brawl
And the Judalon Affair

"I don't know what you mean."

"I'm just from King's. Colonel Wells and Dr. Maddox have had an open quarrel. The colonel called the doctor a blackard to his face, in public! There'll be a challenge without question."

"When did it happen?"

"Not an hour ago. Oh, it's the Vidalia Sand Bar for certain!" Pleased by the surprise he had created; Philippe shook his reins and was off.

Bowie galloped hard toward the city. As he rode up to Connelly's, Andrew Marschalk's tall, dry figure in a carriage driven by a young black boy awaited. The veteran editor was in front of the inn and shook hands with gravity.

"A bad business, this," he said.

"Just what occurred?" asked Bowie.

"Dr. Maddox sent a challenge to Montfort Wells as a result of their misunderstanding. Colonel Samuel Wells intercepted and took it as a personal affront, offering to give satisfaction himself."

They entered the taproom. At the bar, snorting and drinking heavily, was Colonel Wells, who said to Andrew Marschalk, "Have you made representations to my opponent, sir?"

"I have, Colonel," said Marschalk gravely.

"His reply?"

"I confess I have not yet obtained his agreement. But I came anyway, hoping I might find here greater forbearance and wisdom."

Colonel Wells said angrily, "You ask me to accept what Maddox has rejected, sir? That man meant to murder my brother! Montfort is an old

142   **J. Wayne Frye**

man, sir, nearly blind. If I held back now, I'd deserve the epithet not only of coward but fool."

The colonel's liquor was working on him and his close-set eyes were red with fury. General Cuny, the ready diplomat, intervened. "May I beseech one member of this party to agree to a provision which may mitigate these unhappy circumstances?" His eye was on Bowie. "It is to you, sir that I appeal."

"Why to me?" Bowie said in surprise.

"Your disagreement with Major Norris Wright, sir. I fear it might have tragic consequences if either of you were present on this field. May I have your word to remain away from the duelling ground?"

"You've suggested this, may I ask, to Major Wright?"

"Yes, sir."

"And he?"

"Agreed, I am happy to say. Provided you agree also."

"If Major Wright agrees, I can hardly do otherwise."

Marschalk thanked him and departed stately and composed. Meanwhile, the tension in the room was palatable. It was almost like awaiting a declaration of war.

In the negotiations between the seconds that evening Bowie took no part. Judge Crain and Al Blanchard represented Maddox and General Cuny and Major McWherters spoke for Wells. The meeting was coldly formal, and terms which could have been foreseen were agreed upon. The place would be the Vidalia Sand Bar. The weapons would be pistols at twelve paces. The referee would be Andrew Marschalk.

On one point only was there disagreement. Thrice the seconds conferred with their principals before it was settled. Dr. Maddox wished the meeting set off for a week, asserting that he had certain business affairs to settle. However, it was decided that the challenge had been delivered on the fifteenth of September. The meeting was set for the nineteenth, four days later.

The word next morning was that Major Wright had left Natchez, gone down-river not to return, at least for some time. To Rezin this was pure relief. He was anxious over his brother, not so much for fear of any formal encounter, but because there was no telling what might happen if Bowie and Wright met accidentally. A killing might even occur under circumstances that could be interpreted as murder, and the grave penalties of the law invoked. With Wright gone, he felt free to return to Arcadia and urged Jim to accompany him.

"Not right now," Bowie said.

"Why, Jim?"

Jim was vague. "A matter or two I've got to settle."

Rezin studied the floor, not looking at Jim as he said, "Women are chancy creatures. They have a whole different universe of ideas and standards and ways of doing things. A man can understand everything there is to know about men, and still not know the first thing about women."

It was obvious to Jim which woman he was talking about. "Wish you'd come to the point."

"I am. One of the constant surprises in life is the way the least kind of a woman can twist the biggest, grandest man around her little finger. I've seen a tree," Rezin continued, "a hundred foot to the first branch it stood, without a knot or gnarly place on it. You'd think nothing could harm that tree, except maybe a lightning blast from heaven. But it was dead. Why? Because of a little, weak vine. The vine couldn't even stand by itself, but it had twisted its soft arms around the tree, and climbed up the perfect trunk as if it loved the tree and wanted its protection and company. And all the time it was choking the life out of the tree, until the great tree was nothing but a dead stub with the vine still clinging with its arms about it, still blooming and green, still smiling and to all the world still innocent and loving."

"No use pretending I don't understand you," Jim said. "You're meaning Judalon."

"Yes, I am."

"Then you're stepping where you've got no right to walk, Rezin."

Rezin said no more. He took his saddlebags and left the inn to ride down to the ferry at the foot of Silver Street.

Bowie hated himself for talking like that to Rezin, and for the calm submission with which his brother took it.

Jim Bowie: The Vidalia Sandbar Brawl
And the Judalon Affair

It was speedily evident that the delay in the Wells-Maddox duel would have unpleasing results. Natchez found itself possessed of two armed camps, and it was difficult to keep from involvement with one side or the other. A man referred to the quarrel guardedly, if at all, even to his closest friends. The ladies found matters especially bewildering and annoying. One had to display such tiresome adroitness in treading the narrow way between the bothersome hostile parties. Social life was virtually suspended, and the fair element agreed fervently that it would be an enormous relief when the business was over.

For Bowie, the days passed heavily and slowly. His thoughts were not clear and manageable; new forces aroused in him and distracted him. Sometimes he lay fully dressed on his bed, staring at the ceiling. Sometimes he played idly and silently at various games of chance with some companion in the taproom, drinking more than was good for him. Sometimes he walked alone beside the brink of the bluff, scarcely seeing the magnificence of the river below him, or went equally blindly through the town.

On such a walk as this, the day before the impending duel, he recognized, near the City Market, the fine horses belonging to the Duncan's. At some indefinable call of instinct he quickened his pace and when he saw Judalon among the market stalls, he was elated. Her head, on this morning, was bare, and she wore a wide-flowing dress of jade-green almost translucent. She did not

J. Wayne Frye

see him at first, being busy filling a large market basket, which the Duncan's' black coachman bore behind her.

When he was almost beside her, she cried out as if startled, "Jim! What are you doing here?" She dismissed the butler and said to Jim, "I am grateful that you kept your promise."

He said, "You know it's a torment for me not to see you."

"You'll hear it soon enough, so I'll tell you. Philippe and I had it out." She made a small grimace of distaste. "I hate scenes and he wept, begged, promised, but I convinced him it is over between us. He's gone to stay at the inn."

"When did this happen, Judalon?"

"This morning. Be patient, as I will soon be a free woman."

He watched her shimmering jade-green figure go through the passageways between the market stalls until it disappeared.

The first person he saw when he returned to Connelly's was Philippe Cabanal. He was standing alone by the taproom bar, and he was very drunk.

Bowie stopped in the doorway. Never had he beheld such a change in man as had come over Philippe. It was as if a mask had been torn from his face. All pretence at pride and respectability was gone; he had the look of a kicked dog, his face fallen in, his clothes disarranged and soiled with food and liquor. He appeared a man who had given up on life.

Jim Bowie: The Vidalia Sandbar Brawl
And the Judalon Affair

What could he say to the man? Bowie had been angered at Philippe, had despised him. At this minute he came near being contrite toward him.

"Sit down, Jim." Philippe pulled at his sleeve. For a moment Bowie resisted. But as the other almost fell into a chair, calling for brandy, he took a seat across the table. A waiter brought a bottle and glasses.

"What are you doing here at Connelly's?" Bowie asked.

"Livin' here. Gotta room. That son-of-a-bitch Wright? He's broken up my home. You wanna know what's going on? Well, I'll tell you. Because it was a plot between him and my wife. Norris Wright and my wife!"

"What kind of a plot?"

"Divorce. Throw me out on my ear."

Bowie's hand closed on the other's arm.

"Wright planned that with her?"

"Wha' you think? Gone to New Orleans has he? What for do you suppose? Why to put the act through the legislature for a divorce. Cause of the church that's the only way to get a divorce. "

Bowie sat back. Some things were suddenly clear. That was why Wright departed the very day after the Maddox-Wells quarrel. Why he was so willing to agree not to go to the field for the duel provided Bowie agreed.

It had been the very day after Judalon herself announced to Bowie her decision to divorce Philippe. Bowie had let her wheedle him into blundering out once more his love to her, making him promise not to call out Norris Wright, because Norris Wright was the man she meant to marry all the time. Cold fury filled him at the woman and at the man.

The day of the duel dawned clear and somewhat warm. Contrary to the usual custom, the meeting was to take place at high noon. Connelly's was a bustle of warlike preparation, which included not a little alcoholic fortification. Already, by ten o'clock, the bluffs overlooking the river were crowded and onlookers, not a few of them women, filled the galleries at Connelly's. From this vantage point the long low island could be seen clearly across the river, and many hoped to glimpse something of the proceedings. A telescope or two were in evidence.

At eleven o'clock, Bowie rode down to the landing and saw his friends aboard the steam ferry which would take them to the sand bar. There were five in the party: General Cuny and Major McWherters, seconds; Jefferson Wells, witness; Dr. Cuny, surgeon and Colonel Samuel Wells, principal. The principal was perhaps the coolest of them. He smiled as Bowie squeezed his hand with a fervent wish of good luck.

The Maddox party was crossing in a boat chartered for the purpose. There were five of them also: the seconds, Judge Crain and Al Blanchard; Carey Blanchard, witness; Dr. Denny, surgeon; and Dr. Thomas Maddox, principal. Andrew Marschalk, as referee, had preceded both parties to the sand bar.

Jim Bowie: The Vidalia Sandbar Brawl
And the Judalon Affair

When Bowie rode back toward the inn, he observed that the crowd on the bluff was growing greater. A burly figure, with one eye glued to a long brass telescope was none other than Bloody Jack Sturdevant. Near him was another interesting figure. Bowie pulled up his horse and looked down at the man. "Philippe," he said. "Come back up to the inn with me."

Philippe shook his head. "Got a little speculation here, Sturdevant and me. We think we can make out with the telescope what's going to happen. I've got a hundred on Maddox."

"Where did you get the money?"

"Borrowed it." His eye strayed to Sturdevant.

Bowie said, "You'll lose that bet."

"It may interest you that Maddox has been doing his pistol work regularly the last four days."

Bowie did not hear him. He was looking up the street where a horseman sat on his mount, his attitude one of concentrated thought as he watched the ferryboat churn across the river. It was Norris Wright. He was back in Natchez, after saying he'd be gone until after the duel. He observed him boarding a skiff to the sand bar. Bowie struck his hands together. "I knew it! That relieves me of my promise."

In the side pocket of his coat, Bowie had a loaded pistol. The tails of the garment covered the sheathed knife at his hip. He quickly headed to the shore to hire a skiff to the sand bar.

The sequence of events set off by his bit of gossip concerning Montfort Wells had been upsetting to Dr. Thomas Maddox. Since he had been challenged, the days had been a strain to him, and although he had spent them in assiduous practice with the pistol, he felt none of the confidence in himself that Philippe Cabanal had expressed to Bowie. Too late, however, to do anything but face the consequences. Somewhat pale, but fully determined, he did so.

He had removed his long coat and stood watching Judge Crain examine the pistol he was to use. It was a strange weapon supplied by the referee, Andrew Marschalk. Maddox wished very much that he might have used the pistol with which he had fired so many rounds at the white target under the tutelage of Judge Crain and Al Blanchard.

They stood in a sandy clearing, screened by trees and brush from the river and the nearer shore. The seconds and others formed two groups, on either side of the line of fire. Already the coin had been tossed and positions selected. There really was little to choose since the sun was directly overhead and the ground perfectly level.

"This way, Tom," said Judge Crain.

A hand was on the doctor's arm. He felt himself guided forward a few steps and placed in position. At twelve paces, a distance which seemed brutally close, he saw the bitter features and close-set eyes of Colonel Wells. Beside Wells stood General Cuny who looked at Judge Crain and the judge silently returned the look. There was bad blood between the chief seconds.

Jim Bowie: The Vidalia Sandbar Brawl
And the Judalon Affair

Maddox felt a heavy weight in his hand. The pistol had been placed there by Crain. Vaguely he glanced down at it. Hammer cocked. He had only to pull the trigger.

Blood pounded in his ears as he turned his right side toward his antagonist, to give as narrow a target as possible.

Andrew Marschalk said, "Are you ready, gentlemen?"

Maddox nodded. Wells nodded. Marschalk stepped back.

Now it was coming. Death awaited one of them, maybe both.

Dry, mechanical voice began a count. "Make ready: one, two, three."

Maddox's hand was jolted by the recoil of his weapon. A puff of grey smoke obscured his enemy. Even in the dull solid shock of the almost simultaneous twin reports he heard the sinister hum close by his head. Smoke drifted aside. Both men still were erect: neither touched.

Maddox experienced great disappointment. If he had only drawn a little blood from Wells, the thing would be over and they could both go home. Judge Crain, General Cuny and Andrew Marschalk were in a short, stiff conference. Another shot must be exchanged.

Once more Maddox took his place. Once more he saw the grim visage of Colonel Wells facing him. Once more Marschalk began the measured count. The two shots thudded almost together. And still neither man had been hit.

J. Wayne Frye

Jim Bowie: The Vidalia Sandbar Brawl
And the Judalon Affair

In a daze, Maddox saw Marschalk step between them. "Gentlemen, I compliment you both on carrying yourselves in a manner to excite every admiration." The journalist smiled. "Now, since the most rigid interpretation of the code enjoins no third shot after two have been exchanged, I earnestly pray that this difference be forgotten and a reconciliation take place which will be of profound satisfaction to the multitude of friends you both possess."

With gratitude, Dr. Maddox heard these words. The black hole in the muzzle of Colonel Wells' pistol had looked uncommonly huge and close. He gave a nod. To his intense relief, Wells also indicated a willingness to end the quarrel. The two men came together to shake hands.

In that moment they all saw Major Norris Wright making his way through the bushes toward them, pushing aside the branches with his gold-headed sword cane.

Surprise in Marschalk's face turned to coldness. Intense silence fell.

"Sir," the editor said stiffly, "I must say that I had not expected to see you here."

Wright glanced at the Wells contingent, bristling in a close group, with a spiteful gleam.

"The duel is over?" he asked. "I thought I heard the shots. Surely the principals are reconciled.

Marschalk swallowed his strong disapproval. Wright actually had not violated the letter of his agreement. Marschalk's face lit up. "Then I say this is good, very good, a most happy resolution.

Jim Bowie: The Vidalia Sandbar Brawl
And the Judalon Affair

Let us congratulate our principals as much on their good sense in recognizing the moment when both were vindicated as on the courage with which they upheld their honour. We must all be equally happy. I have a little surprise. In the hope that we might reach this very solution, I took the liberty of bringing a wicker of food and drink over with me. It is here beside these bushes."

Nobody could exceed Marschalk in charm. He went to the place he had indicated and brought forth a large wicker basket. "Let us open it," he said cordially. "The sun is now past the meridian, and what can we do more pleasing than turn what began as a grim occasion into a festive one and drink to each other's health?"

His manner was irresistible. Stiffness melted. Faces relaxed. Men who had not shaken hands in months did so now.

The kindly old gentleman lifted the wickers lid. He began distributing to them fried chicken and sandwiches, and produced glasses into which he poured an excellent wine. As they ate, even General Cuny and Judge Crain became almost genial.

Andrew Marschalk believed he had brought about permanent peace among the men present. Now he thought he saw a chance to heal still another wound through the opportune arrival of Norris Wright. He would be wrong.

J. Wayne Frye

Jim Bowie: The Vidalia Sandbar Brawl
And the Judalon Affair

Chapter 8
A Mystery All These Years

"I consider, Major," Andres Marschalk began, "that this is a fitting occasion to bring about friendly relations between yourself and James Bowie, whom you must acknowledge is a gentleman."

For once he had uttered an unfortunate remark. Wright stepped back as if he had been struck, his face paling with anger. "I acknowledge no such thing!" he exclaimed.

With consternation, Marschalk saw his careful planning undone and made one desperate suggestion. "But you will shake his hand?"

Wright appeared to be intensely agitated. "Never! May I be struck dead, if I ever touch that scoundrel's hand in friendship!"

The words still hung quivering on the air when all present heard the crackle of branches. Bending low to avoid the low-swinging boughs, Bowie, who had taken a skiff over to the sandbar, stepped into the clearing, obviously having overheard Wright's tirade of anger. Jim halted, face set, looking at Wright with intense disdain on his face. Yet, it would be neither of these two who set off the coming explosion.

Gentleman's duelling etiquette was about to be unceremoniously tossed aside. With a sudden reckless movement, Judge Crain snatched from his coat pocket a short-barrelled pistol. General Cuny's face grew ashen with fear, then taut with ferocity, as he tugged to get his weapon out, which had caught in his garment.

"You and I can settle our differences right now," Crain said fiercely.

Bowie heard the double click of the hammer as it was cocked, saw the judge's pistol come up, and stupidly stepped between Crain and the general, who still was tearing helplessly for his imprisoned weapon.

Things were happening rapidly as all hell broke loose, but the truth is to each one there it was as if everything was in slow motion. One can live an eternity in the moment, as the doors of infinity open wide to the soul. Thus, there is a gloriousness that lives in the slow motion, a realization that time itself is a great gift and that in the blink of an eye time can run out. It was this kind of movement that spoke of a mind married perfectly to itself and the world around it, confident, focused and reverent.

Movement should always be progress, and that takes the effort of real consideration. Movement can be the random swing of a knife or the precision of the surgeon with a scalpel and in Jim's case he was a skilled surgeon with his knife, so skilled that the mere mention of his name would make men think twice before challenging him. Major Wright made the mistake of challenging him, but he knew that Jim was now off guard, agitated over the treatment of his friend General Cuny being shown disrespect in duelling etiquette from Judge Crain.

Jim Bowie: The Vidalia Sandbar Brawl
And the Judalon Affair

Already Crain's finger was pulling the trigger. A report echoed about the sandbar. Bowie, making the mistake of stepping between the combatants felt a jolt in his hip. His leg seemed suddenly to lose its strength, no longer able to support him. With a sensation of surprise, he found himself falling and knew he was hit.

Prostrate, he watched General Cuny free his pistol at last, cock it and fire. The judge winced from a wound in his arm, the same arm the general had wounded once before.

Crain threw down his empty weapon, drew a second pistol, and coldly fired at his old enemy again.

General Cuny reeled slowly in a circle and went down. With a cry his brother, the little doctor, ran over to him.

Bowie shook his head to clear it and began levering himself up, pushing with his hands on the ground and dragging his wounded leg. He was erect, desperately clutching for his own pistol. He took it out, cocked and pulled the trigger at Judge Crain, but his wound unsteadied him. The shot went wild.

Reports of other pistols sounded about him. He hardly knew who fired or at whom. To one side, as if he had no part in the melee, stood Norris Wright, leaning on his gold-headed cane. Time to settle with him later thought Jim. Bowie wrenched from the sheath on his hip the great knife, and setting his teeth because of his pain, began to hobble across the sand toward Crain.

Jim Bowie: The Vidalia Sandbar Brawl
And the Judalon Affair

The judge saw a wild man closing on him. With all his strength he dashed his empty pistol in Bowie's face, and ran, clutching his wounded arm. He need not have fled so rapidly because his heavy weapon struck the round knob of its handle on Bowie's forehead. Stunned, Jim again fell to the ground. For a moment he lay there, trying to shake off the blackness that threatened to overwhelm him. He turned on his side, his head aching from the blow, acute pain shooting in his wounded hip.

Someone cried out a panic warning. With clearing vision Bowie saw it. Norris Wright had drawn from his cane the long, sharp sword it concealed. Throwing the cane aside, his narrow face murderous, he rushed upon Bowie with the blade. Everyone watched, struck motionless. Bowie was prostrate, apparently helpless, before the venomous thrust. All were too far from him to render assistance, and who would have dared considering the state of things and the animosity that was as thick as molasses.

With the peculiar fascination of one who sees certain doom approaching, Jim's eyes fixed themselves on the gleaming needle point as it plunged toward his breast. Sharp, tearing pain riddled through his body as Wright rammed it deeper into Jim's body. Wright tugged. It was fixed. He could not get it out. He swore and pulled and pulled. Each effort sent a sickening flush of agony through the man on the ground. He clamped his jaws to keep back his cry of pain. But the

J. Wayne Frye

tough muscles held the blade. Wright could not draw it out.

Furious, the major put a brutal foot on the prostrate body and dragged at the sword once more. The handle came off in his grip, but the steel remained in Bowie's breast.

From Wright came another wild curse, but for a different cause. A great hand closed on his wrist. Instinct sent him into a terrified backward leap. But it was as if an iron shackle had gripped his arm. He felt himself jerked forward, stumbled to his knees, and fell across the bloody body of his enemy. Momentarily, in the sun, Bowie's knife glittered brilliantly. The knife sat defiantly in Jim's hand as if it was an extension of him, an extension of his heart, his soul, his very being. Knife and man were one.

As Wright struggled to free himself from Jim's grip, Jim pulled him closer with his right hand while his weapon of death was in his left hand. A cry arose from Norris Wright, as Jim plunged the knife into his side again and again. Wright stared at Jim with disbelief. Death was written all over Wright's face as if to say to Jim, "You bastard, you have killed me."

It ended in a choke of blood. Norris Wright took a deep breath, collapsed onto Jim and died. For a moment Bowie lay still. Then he rolled the corpse aside, pushed himself up from the ground, and staggered to his feet. Blood smeared and spattered him, his own and that of his enemy. The steel blade still projected from his body.

Jim Bowie: The Vidalia Sandbar Brawl
And the Judalon Affair

Although it had seemed like hours, seemed to be in slow motion, the whole episodic brawl took less than two minutes.

For a moment Jim tried unsteadily to pull out the sword blade. Then he gave up and glared about.

The bloody spectre of death was all about. Two men already lay dead. Everyone was sure Jim had a mortal wound, but everyone knew he was deadly dangerous until the moment he died.

Twenty feet away, tall Alfred Blanchard fired at him as he raced forward. The bullet struck Bowie's left arm, its shock spinning him half around to face the charging Blanchard. Jim recovered, and dragging his wounded leg, leaped toward the man who had fired on him. The sudden thudding of other reports penetrated the air. Pungent powder smoke prickled the nostrils while Bowie's blade, dark with blood, made a sweeping arc. Blanchard staggered backward with a great bloody gash in his right arm, ripped by the razor edge of Bowie's fierce weapon.

More shots. Carey Blanchard snapped a pistol at Bowie, who stood with two feet of steel in his body, ready to collapse. Major McWherters fired, his bullet chipping the younger Blanchard's shoulder. Bowie felt himself falling again, blackness sweeping over him.

As Bowie lay there he heard voices. Someone said, "Turn him over. The point seems to have struck his breastbone and glanced. No, I believe it did not enter the body cavity. Passed along his ribs under the muscle. Here's the point. It extends

160   **J. Wayne Frye**

slightly through the skin at the back. Explains why Wright couldn't get that blade out of him. I shall have difficulty, even with the forceps."

Bowie opened his eyes. Blur. Then he saw a face, a round fat face. Dr. Cuny bending over him. Others looking down also.

"The general?" Bowie said faintly.

"My brother is dead."

"I hoped."

"The carotid artery was severed. Impossible to stop the haemorrhaging."

Dry, professional voice. In this moment the little doctor had a strange dignity.

"Sorry, so sorry!" winched Jim.

"Ease him to his side. Jim, I must hurt you."

Long, shuddering flame of pain.

Cuny, "There it is."

Another voice, "Miracle it didn't kill him."

Bowie's eyes fluttered open again, seeing Andrew Marschalk's austere face, intense with concern. Between podgy fingers Dr. Cuny held the bloody blade of the sword cane.

"Cold metal," the doctor said. "Bent when it collided with the sternum."

Bowie's eyes closed. More pain. Probe and scalpel. Two bullets to remove. Medicines and bandages.

"We must get him across the river."

Voices, many voices about him faint and still and murmuring as night settled thickly.

Bowie healed very slowly. He had lost a lot of blood, and there was an infection which seemed to devour his system. He hardly remembered when he was taken home to Arcadia. After the fight on the island there were days of sinking when he could hardly breathe, days when he was conscious only of distorted figures and voices not understood, days when pain was fresh and blinding. Then came a confused recollection of an interminable jolting progression, when he fought to keep back the moans that welled up from his deeply lacerated chest. This was succeeded by welcome ease, his breath no longer choked, and an immense lassitude when he had not the resolution to turn his gaunt head on the pillow. But when mid-December came, bitter cold, though still weak and far under his usual weight, he was recovered enough to go out in all kinds of weather, yet found it pleasant still to sit in the warm chimney corner. At this time from his brother John came a letter: *Dear James: I have heard how you have been sick and it must be bad for one of your usual health and spirits. The Natchez fight is all over Arkansas, all over the entire country. You are famous, so that I shine by your reflected glory. When you are strong, why not come to Helena? Wife and I will pleasure in seeing you & there is bear & deer for your sport.*

The notoriety of which John wrote was pervasive. Of this the newspapers were palpable proof. Bowie had seen clippings from all over. Rezin was making a collection of them, and it was he who pointed out that though the versions varied amazingly as to details, they were unanimous in one respect: that Bowie was the central, gory figure in the Vidalia Sand Bar affair. One paragraph in Andrew Marschalk's article in the *Herald* struck this keynote: *It was Bowie, terrible and bloody, scorning wounds, a steel shard protruding from his chest, yet striding in spite of a crippled leg, with berserk fury into the teeth of pistol fire, animated only by his deadly ferocity, which drove the Crain party into retreat. To the beholder he seemed almost superhuman: a terrifying and invincible Achilles, an avenging demon, the knife he wielded like a modern Excalibur, irresistible against any human defence.*

The newspapers voiced an interest that was universal and profound. Every detail of the incident had been discussed in countless cabins, hunters' camps, taprooms, steamboat lounges and even sophisticated drawing rooms. In the first weeks after Bowie was brought home, people stood for hours outside the house, staring as if trying to see through its walls. A few lank-haired countrymen even pushed to the door and were indignant when denied the sight of him, as if he were an exhibit in some museum.

From Rezin he learned that all the men involved in the duel, save Andrew Marschalk, had left Natchez. The land syndicate had liquidated its holdings, distributed to each partner his share, and the whole future plan of speculative moves was abandoned. Rezin brought one other piece of news when he returned from Natchez: Philippe Cabanal had gone back to his wife.

Jim Bowie: The Vidalia Sandbar Brawl
And the Judalon Affair

"Nothing much she could do but take him back," Rezin said. "Norris Wright was getting the divorce for her through the legislature. If he'd lived, the act for separation of bodies might have passed, and she would have been free. But the divorce died with Norris Wright."

So Bowie had killed that man, only to drive Judalon back into Philippe's arms.

"They've taken a house and are now living permanently in Natchez," Rezin said, "having disposed of their New Orleans residence. It's for the best. It seems bitter and hard and endless, but you can get over it. A man like you sets his heart on a thing and holds to it. But you can get over this woman."

He said nothing. What was there to say? He would get over her, yes. He would indeed.

He and Judalon would never cross paths again, as Jim would eventually move to Texas where he married aristocratic Ursula Maria de Veramendi in 1831. She died from Cholera in 1833, and Jim would never again find love. In fact, he would go on to greater fame and glory in defence of the Alamo in 1836 where it is postulated by many that he died wielding his knife in one final glorious battle. The knife is assumed to have been taken by one of the victorious Mexican soldiers. Where it is has remained a mystery all these years.

J. Wayne Frye

Jim Bowie: The Vidalia Sandbar Brawl
And the Judalon Affair

Epilogue
I Called It Being Smart

The Vidalia Sandbar Brawl, which took place on September 19, 1827, was the most famous ninety seconds in western history up until October 26, 1881 when the gunfight at OK Corral between the Earp's and the Clanton's supplanted it.

The Day's Scoreboard

Wells Side	Maddox Side	Roles	Injuries
Samuel Wells	Dr. Tom Maddox	Duellists	No injuries
Major McWorter	Judge Crain	Second	Crain shot
Dr. R. Cuny	Dr. J. Denny	Surgeons	Denny hurt
Jim Bowie	A. Blanchard	Supporter	Badly hurt
General Cuny	C. Blanchard	Supporter	Cuny killed
Jeff Wells	Norris Wright	Supporter	Wright killed

I have tried to be as objective as possible in laying out the details of what led up to the sandbar brawl and what actually occurred on that faithful day. However, I must confess to being one who is unable to sincerely like Jim Bowie for the same reason I find it difficult to have any affinity for people like Thomas Jefferson, John Adams and Benjamin Franklin who had the nerve to actually say in the Declaration of Independence that all men are created equal while owning slaves. Even George Washington, America's first President, owned 317 slaves with his wife for work on their plantation at Mount Vernon. Hypocrisy is a trait that was prevalent at the beginning of America, and unfortunately is still highly prevalent in today's America. Still, one cannot help but admire the true grit of men like Jim Bowie. Myself, I have always gone by the adage that the coward lives to fight another day. I am afraid I would not have been suited for the code of honour practiced by duellists during that era in America. When I had the misfortune to be in the U.S. Army during the Vietnam War, when volunteers were requested, rather than stepping forward I stepped back. Coward? Maybe? I called it being smart.

The End

SOME OTHER WAYNE FRYE
HISTORICAL ADVENTURES

(1) How Hockey Saved a Jew From the Holocaust:
The Rudi Ball Story
(2) Worth Part 1
(3) Worth Part 2
(4) Worth Part 3
(5) Canadian Nurses in Times of Peril
(6) Points of Rebellion:
North American Aboriginals
Who Fought for Justice
(7)The Riches of Religion
And the Promotion of Ignorance
(8) Trumped in America

Don't miss his fiction adventures featuring demon hunter Lynton Viñas, and private eyes Aaron Adams and Chablis Louise Chavez.

J. Wayne Frye

Jim Bowie: The Vidalia Sandbar Brawl
And the Judalon Affair

Sources

Batson, James L. (1992). James Bowie and the Sandbar Fight; Birth of the James Bowie Legend & Bowie Knife. Madison, Alabama: Batson Engineering and Metals

Braily, Ron (April 19, 2004), *Remember the Alamo: The Persistence of Myth*, George Mason University History News Network

Davis, William C. (1998). Three Roads to the Alamo: The Lives and Fortunes of David Crockett, James Bowie, and William Barret Travis. New York: HarperCollins. pp 209–219 and associated notes

Bornay Archives at Louisiana State University. Rare Book Archives from 1888

Flayderman, Norm (2004). The Bowie Knife : Unsheathing an American Legend. Lincoln, R.I: Andrew Mowbray. Chapter 10: The Defining Moments: The Sandbar Fight

Hopewell, Clifford (1994). James Bowie Texas Fighting Man: A Biography. Austin, TX: Eakin Press. Chapter 5: Battle of the Sandbar

The Adventures of Jim Bowie (1956). TV Series. Internet Archives from American Broadcasting Company

**Jim Bowie: The Vidalia Sandbar Brawl
And the Judalon Affair**

The Avoyelles Pelican: Marksville, Louisiana
Archives

Welman, I.M. (1951). Bowie and the Mistress.
Reading Essentials Publishing 2009
Republication

J. Wayne Frye

Jim Bowie: The Vidalia Sandbar Brawl
And the Judalon Affair

www.ingramcontent.com/pod-product-compliance
Lightning Source LLC
Chambersburg PA
CBHW061723020426
42331CB00006B/1060